LOGIA OF
DEBTOR-CREDITOR RELATIONS LAW

LOGIA OF
DEBTOR-CREDITOR RELATIONS LAW

Rodney D. Chrisman

Bedford, Virginia
2013

For my children, grandchildren,
and descendants to a thousand generations,
may you trust always in the Lord Jesus Christ, the Master debt-payer,
and serve Him faithfully Who redeemed you at the price of His Own blood.

▌ PUBLISHER'S PREFACE

"Logia" is the English transliteration of the Greek word "λόγια," which is translated "oracles." This word is used four times in the New Testament. Stephen uses this word in his famous speech in *Acts* 7:38 when he tells the audience that Moses "received the living oracles ["λόγια"] to give unto us." Paul uses it in *Romans* 3:2 when he notes of the Jews "that unto them were committed the oracles ["λόγια"] of God." Peter uses it when he writes that "[i]f any man speak, let him speak as the oracles ["λόγια"] of God." 1 *Peter* 4:11. Finally, the writer of Hebrews uses logia when he castigates his readers for their becoming dull of hearing and not progressing to being teachers as they ought have been by that time (*Hebrews* 5:12-14). He instead states that they needed someone to teach them "the first principles of the oracles ["λόγια"] of God." *Hebrews* 5:12.

In each of the passages described above, "logia" is used to refer to the authoritative pronouncements of the Lord God, including pronouncements in both the Old and New Testament eras. This word, and the corresponding belief that Scripture contains the authoritative pronouncements or logia of God for all areas of life, inspired the name of the publisher, Logia Press, LLC, and this book, Logia of Contracts Law. God has spoken His logia. May his people seek to understand and apply His logia in every sphere of life for His glory alone.

Logia Press, LLC
Bedford, VA
August, 2013

AUTHOR'S PREFACE AND ACKNOWLEDGEMENTS

The Purpose of the Book

This book is written to help paralegal students learn to apply the Christian worldview to debtor-creditor relations law issues. It is certainly not complete. Much more could be said about every topic, and for every topic likely hundreds more could be considered. Thus, the hope is not a comprehensive treatment of the Christian worldview of contracts law (as laudable as that goal would be.) Rather, this book is written with the more modest goal of exposing the students to the application of the Christian worldview to contracts law in an interesting way that might equip them to continue the practice of the application of that worldview to other issues that they encounter in their lives. The Bible is authoritative for all things to which it speaks, and it speaks to all things.

The Approach of this Book

With the broad purpose stated, I thought it appropriate to state a word about the approach of the book. One of things that I liked best about law school and the practice of law were the interesting cases. The facts of the cases that one encounters in practice and in law school are often very memorable. The writing of certain judges can also be engaging and fascinating. Therefore, I have chosen, for the most part, to structure this book, like the other Logia Press titles, around a number of carefully chosen cases that raise topics that I want us to think through together. I hope that you find the cases as interesting and enjoyable as I have.[1]

The materials following the cases are designed to help you apply the Christian worldview to the case and related topics. Sometimes I attempt a resolution of a particular issue. Other times I do not (or, perhaps, cannot.) The application of a biblical worldview to the complex legal issues of our day is, to distort an old saying, a row that only a few are hoeing. Since few Christian scholars are working in this area in our time, the task to which we shall set ourselves in this book is made all the harder. But, perhaps as a result of this, any successes that God may grant us to enjoy may be all the sweeter.

Finally, as to the approach, I will also include questions that are meant to further stimulate your thought and possibly provide fodder for discussion. Sometimes these questions may cause us to reconsider items that have long been a part of the American legal and commercial systems. This can be somewhat uncomfortable. However, we should not shy away from this important work. Nothing, even by long use and custom, can become good if God's word condemns it.

A Word as to Judges, Authors, Cases, and Other Materials Cited

Lawyers cite and argue from authorities. Thus, a critical skill for a lawyer, and indeed any person, to develop is the ability to evaluate, distinguish, critique, and learn from various authorities. To that end, I cite a number of cases written by various judges, and I cite materials written by various authors, some of which I would agree with and some of which I would not.

Hopefully this will not be surprising. If this were a book about constitutional law, I would have you read *Roe v. Wade*. Certainly, writing from a Christian worldview, the fact that I would have you read that case would not cause you to draw the conclusion that I agree with everything in it. (The fact is that I agree with very little in it, and I think it is one of the most despicable opinions ever written.) We would read the case, not because we agree with it, but because we do not and it is a part of the legal (and indeed political) fabric of modern America. Many of the materials and authorities quoted, cited, and used in this book are selected for similar reasons.

Therefore, the inclusion of materials in this book, including the cases, should not be construed as an approval or endorsement of the judge, author, or arguments presented merely because of their inclusion in the

---

[1] I deviate from this practice more in this book than the other Logia Press titles due primarily to the topics involved. Some of the topics, such as whether debt is sin and bankruptcy biblical, are not addressed in cases but are essential for our consideration of Debtor-Creditor Relations Law.

text. Further, agreement with a judge or author on one point should not be construed as an endorsement of that author on all points. Rather, discernment is needed—and, in my opinion, required. You may not agree with me on all points, and likely you will not. Nor would I likely agree with you on all points. We should be able to state our arguments clearly and even forcefully to one another, and yet remain friends or colleagues. It seems to me that "love your neighbor" requires in this setting that we deal fairly with each argument offered, noting areas of agreement and disagreement, in a professional manner. Further, we should extend that same respect and love to the authors and judges whose materials are contained herein.

My Approach in Editing of Cases

I have edited the cases contained in this book. If you look these cases up in their full glory, you will likely want to write me and thank me for this. Cases, particularly U.S. Supreme Court cases, tend to be bloated with argumentation and citations that are tedious even for lawyers to read. In fact, many modern Supreme Court cases seemed designed to weary the reader into submission as opposed to winning him over with persuasive argument. I have attempted to spare you the ordeal of being wearied by the sheer number of words alone.

Generally, I have followed the normal editing conventions, such as indicating deleted and inserted material. Deleted material I usually indicated with ellipses or ***. Inserted material is set apart in brackets. Footnotes are often deleted without any indication, as are most citations to other authorities. When footnotes are included, they are typically renumbered in conformity with the numbering used in the book. At times minor corrections, additions, and changes have been made without any indication whatsoever. Further, many grammatical and some spelling errors are left in the cases as they appear in the originals. Language changes over time, and court opinions are no exceptions. Of course, if you have questions about what has been deleted or added, I would direct you to the actual opinions for comparison, as they are freely available from a number of sources on the Internet.

Acknowledgments and Thanks

As always, I would like to thank my lovely bride, Heather, for her love, companionship, support, and editing assistance. I could not begin to express how much she means to me and how indebted I am to her. Her worth is indeed far above rubies, and she does me good and not evil all the days of my life.

Obviously, all the mistakes, whether grammatical, typographical, conceptual, or otherwise, remain my own.

And, last but not least, I thank you for reading and studying the book. I hope you grow in your understanding of and love for the law and, more importantly, the Lord who created it.

Soli Deo Gloria

Rodney D. Chrisman
Bedford, VA
August, 2013

TABLE OF CONTENTS

Publisher's Preface ....*v*
Author's Preface and Acknowledgments .... *vii*
Contents ....*xi*

Chapter 1.
Toward a Biblical View of Debt 1

Chapter 2.
A Law-of-Nature Framework for
Analyzing Commercial Law Issues 13

Chapter 3.
A Biblical Analysis of Self-Help Repossession.................................27

Chapter 4.
Is Bankruptcy Biblical?...37

Chapter 5.
The Purposes of Bankruptcy...47

Chapter 6.
Nondischargeability and the Biblical Worldview 55

Chapter 7.
Tithing in Chapter 13 Plans 65

Chapter 8.
The GM Bankruptcy...77

Index *95*

CHAPTER 1
TOWARD A BIBLICAL VIEW OF DEBT

Debt is an important issue in America today. As a people, we are heavily in debt. One need not look far to find news stories discussing the crushing debt carried by most civil governments, from the U.S. federal government down to the local level.[1] Not only are civil governments heavily in debt, so are many churches. We live in an age when church and ministry bankruptcies are all too common.[2] Not surprisingly, individuals and families all over the country are also heavily in debt. The average U.S. household owes $15,325 in credit card debt and $32,041 in student loan debt, not to mention mortgage and auto loans debt.[3]

That said, is all of this debt really a problem? This book considers the biblical worldview of debtor-creditor relations law; accordingly, a recognition of the huge amount of debt in the American economy, and a consideration of the biblical view of debt, are good places to start. Should a follower of Christ incur debt at all or rather strive to be debt-free? If some debt is permissible, what kinds and how much? Is incurring debt a sin against God or is it just a wisdom issue? Should our modern debt systems be viewed as a blessing, much like viewing the concept of money

---

[1] As this book is going to print, the level of federal debt is a huge political and cultural issue. Further, the city of Detroit recently filed for bankruptcy protection. Numerous other examples abound.

[2] The bankruptcy of the Crystal Cathedral in California made national headlines, but numerous other churches and ministries enter bankruptcy every year.

[3] Tim Chen, *American Household Credit Card Debt Statistics: 2013*, NerdWallet Credit Card Blog (n.d.), http://www.nerdwallet.com/blog/credit-card-data/average-credit-card-debt-household/. This blog post has a good methodology of gathering data from several sources and combining it into a useful consumer debt profile.

as a good gift from God, or as a curse that is enslaving and impoverishing the nation?

These are just some of the difficult questions that surround a biblical discussion of debt. These questions, and many others, are discussed in Sunday School classes, seminars, and sermons across the country. Many books have been written on this topic from a Christian perspective. Further, there are ministries devoted to helping Christians deal with these types of questions.

Despite all of this effort, the understanding of what the Bible teaches in this important area varies greatly among God-fearing, Bible-believing Christians. Therefore, this chapter does not hope to offer definitive answers to these questions. Rather, the goal is to provide a framework for considering and discussing them from a Christian worldview. In order to do this, we will first consider whether a Christian should live completely debt-free. Then, we will consider whether there are other biblical principles relating to debt.

Should Christians Live Debt-Free?

This is possibly the most fundamental question with regard to debt: should a Christian live debt-free? The answer to this question impacts not only how a Christian should live, but, arguably, would impact what type of legal system a Christian should look for and seek to implement with regard to borrowing and lender and debtor-creditor relations. There are many answers to this question given by leaders and teachers in the church today. They range from borrowing at all is a sin that should be avoided, to limited borrowing for a limited time is acceptable, to viewing borrowing and lending as a good gift from God as long as it is bounded by certain Christian principles. In the following, a representative example of each of these positions is presented.[4]

Some Christians believe that borrowing at all is sinful and should be avoided. For example, the Institute in Basic Life Principles ("IBLP"), the ministry founded and run by Bill Gothard, teaches that Christians should never borrow money and that borrowing money "violates Scripture."[5] *Men's Manual: Volume 2*, which is published by IBLP and is

---

[4] Doubtless many, many more examples can be given. These are meant to be a mere sample offered to provide fodder for thought and discussion.

[5] Institute in Basic Life Principles, *Men's Manual: Volume* 2 78 (1983). I assume that saying something violates Scripture is the same as saying it is a sin. Perhaps the *Men's Manual* merely means to say that it is unwise, which would certainly be the position of a number of other teachers—debt is not a sin but it is unwise. However, reading the *Men's Manual* materials, I get the distinct impression that it is teaching that debt is a sin. *See also Are There Consequences for Borrowing Money?*, Life Questions section of the Institute in Basic Life Principles Website (n.d.), http://iblp.org/questions/are-there-consequences-borrowing-money (this webpage contains

the companion textbook for IBLP's video series entitled *Financial Freedom*, lists 16 consequences of borrowing. The very first is that it violates Scripture. It states:

> The message of Scripture on borrowing is quite clear: *Do not do it.* God commands Christians to keep out of debt altogether. *"Owe no man any thing, but to love one another . . ." (Romans 13:8).*
>
> *Strong's Exhaustive Concordance* amplifies the message behind these words: "Owe to no one, no not anything, nothing at all."[6]

It goes on to list 15 other consequences of borrowing. For instance, consequence number two is that borrowing "constitutes a judgment of God . . . upon His people for failing to follow His ways."[7] The Scripture cited for this proposition is *Deuteronomy* 28: 15 and 44, which is from the covenant curses, and states:

> But it shall come to pass, if thou wilt not hearken unto the voice of the Lord thy God, to observe to do all his commandments and his statutes which I command thee this day; that all these curses shall come upon thee, and overtake thee . . . . He shall lend to thee, and thou shalt not lend to him: he shall be the head, and thou shalt be the tail.

Other consequences listed include: that borrowing "produces bondage to creditors," based upon *Proverbs* 22:7 (which states that "the borrower is servant to the lender");[8] that "borrowing presumes upon the future," based upon *James* 4:13-14 and *Proverbs* 27:1;[9] and that borrowing "damages God's reputation" because "[w]hen Christians borrow, they are saying to the world, 'God is not taking care of my needs, so I have to make up the difference with a loan.'"[10]

As the foregoing demonstrates, the teaching of Bill Gothard and IBLP seems to be that borrowing is a sin and Christians should not borrow at all. It is viewed as bondage, as against the teachings of Scripture, and as besmirching the reputation of God.

R. J. Rushdoony's teachings on debt seem to agree with IBLP's, with the slight modification that Dr. Rushdoony's teachings seems to

---

very similar information as to what is found in the *Men's Manual: Volume 2* at pages 78-81).

   [6] *Men's Manual: Volume 2, supra*, note 5, at 78 (emphasis in original).
   [7] *Id.* at 79.
   [8] *Id.*
   [9] *Id.*
   [10] *Id.* at 81.

allow room for short-term as opposed to long-term borrowing. In his work on systematic theology, he writes the following of debt.

> Debt, statist and personal, is inflationary and destructive. Solomon said, "The rich ruleth over the poor, and the borrower is servant (or, slave) to the lender" (Prov. 22:7). Debt is bondage, and a premise of ungodly rule. A non-Christian society will be debt-ridden and inflationary. Debt and inflation involve a consumption of the future and a burden on the present.[11]

Further, Dr. Roshdoony has also opined that "God's goal is a debt-free society which is also poverty-free, and this is only possible in terms of His law."[12]

Up to this point, it appears that Dr. Rushdoony would be in full agreement with IBLP's teachings on debt. However, as the following quote reveals, Dr. Rushdoony believed that Scripture did allow for borrowing in certain situations. In *Larceny in the Heart*, he writes:

> The Bible forbids long-term debt and limits debt to six years, and for serious reasons only. The seventh year must be a Sabbath unto the Lord, from debt, among other things (Deut. 15:1-6). As a general rule, we are to "Owe no man anything, but to love one another" (Rom. 13:8). God declares that debt is a form of slavery, and "the borrower is servant (literally, slave) to the lender (Prov. 22:7).
>
> In the modern world, however, debt is a way of life, for not only unbelievers but churchmen, and for churches and Christian organizations. Debt as a way of life has deep rots in sin, in pride, envy, "and covetousness, which is idolatry" (Col. 3:5; cf. Eph. 5:5; 1 Tim. 6:17).
>
> . . .
>
> It becomes apparent why Scripture takes so strong a position on debt: it is a moral and religious issue. *First*, we have seen, debt is basic to inflation, and it is responsible, in all the moral compromise debt involves, for the immorality which marks an inflationary era. *Second*, we are forbidden as Christians to become slaves, and debt is slavery. "Ye are bough with a price: be not ye the servants (or, slaves) of men" (1 Cor. 7:23). *Third*, not only are we God's possession and property, and hence cannot becomes the slaves of men, but

---

[11] R. J. Rushdoony, *Systematic Theology in Two Volumes: Volume II*, 984 (1994).
[12] R. J. Rushdoony, *The Institutes of Biblical Law: Volume One*, 145 (1973).

out time belongs to Him: we cannot mortgage our future to men by means of debt.

To live debt-free, except for emergency conditions, or a short-term (six-year) debt to pay for our house, farm, or business, means *to live providently.*[13]

Accordingly, we see that, while Dr. Rushdoony condemns debt in the strongest possible language, including likening it to sin. He apparently also felt that the Bible permitted borrowing in "emergency conditions, or [for] a short-term (six-year) . . . to pay for our house, farm, or business."[14]

Still, both Bill Gothard and Dr. Roshdoony agree that *Romans* 13:8 is a general prohibition against Christians borrowing. Further, both agree that, based upon *Proverbs* 22:7, debt is a type of slavery. However, they differ in that Dr. Rushdoony sees borrowing in emergency situations and for very short-terms to be acceptable.

In contrast to Dr. Rushdoony and Mr. Gothard, many Christian teachers do not teach that it is a sin for Christians to borrow money. For example, in *Business by the Book*, Larry Burkett writes:

In recent years several well-meaning Christian teachers have stated that borrowing money is not in line with the Bible. That is wrong. I sincerely wish that there were such an instruction in God's Word; it would make teaching on this particular topic much simpler. But borrowing is not scripturally prohibited.[15]

Mr. Burkett then goes on to address the arguments of those he calls "absolutists—those who believe that all borrowing is a sin."[16]

Of most interest for our purposes here is Mr. Burkett's discussion of *Romans* 13:8. He notes that this is the verse most often quoted by the absolutists, but he disagrees with their interpretation of it.[17] Instead of forbidding all borrowing, Mr. Burkett asserts that, in context, the passage is concerned more with taxes due to Rome. "In Romans 13:1 Paul was dealing specifically with the raging debate over whether Christians should pay taxes to the heathen government of Rome. (Sound familiar?) In Romans 13:6–8 Paul was saying to the Christians, 'Don't be left owing anyone anything, even taxes to Rome.'"[18]

---

[13] R. J. Rushdoony, *Larceny in the Heart: The Economics of Satan and the Inflationary State* 75-77 (2002) (emphasis in original).

[14] *Id.* at 77.

[15] Larry Burkett, *Business By The Book: Complete Guide of Biblical Principles for the Workplace* 174 (2006).

[16] *Id.*

[17] *Id.* at 175.

[18] *Id.* at 176.

Even though Mr. Burkett does not think the Bible condemns all borrowing as sin, he still argues that borrowing is risky and biblical wisdom dictates that it should generally be avoided. "Borrowing is not prohibited scripturally, but neither is it encouraged. It is always presented in a negative context and with many warnings about its misuse."[19]

Mr. Burkett then offers what he sees as the "three fundamental scriptural principles related to borrowing." [20] They are: (1) avoid borrowing unless absolutely necessary (based upon the nature of borrowing in general and its associated risks),[21] (2) avoid signing surety on a loan (based upon *Proverbs* 6:1-3),[22] and (3) avoid long-term debt (based upon *Deuteronomy* 15's Sabbatical year teachings).[23] As you can see, these principles are generally consistent with the teachings of Dr. Rushdoony and Mr. Gothard presented above. However, Mr. Burkett presents them as wisdom principles found in Scripture as opposed to outright commands to avoid borrowing. Mr. Burkett argues that the only real biblical commandment with regard to whether to borrow is that one must repay what one owes, derived primarily from *Psalm* 37:21 which states that "The wicked borroweth, and payeth not again: But the righteous sheweth mercy, and giveth."[24]

In *Business for the Glory of God*, Dr. Wayne Grudem goes even farther than Mr. Burkett and argues "that the process of borrowing and lending is another wonderful gift that God has given to us as human beings."[25] Like Mr. Burkett, Dr. Grudem does not believe that the Bible prohibits all borrowing and lending. In discussing *Romans* 13:8, he writes:

> I do not think that Romans 13:8 (" owe no one anything") prohibits all borrowing or even discourages borrowing, for taken in context it simply says we should pay what we owe when we owe it. If we look at the statement in its proper context, translated to show the connection between verse 7 and verse 8 (as is done in the recently published *English Standard Version*), it reads as follows:

>> For the same reason you also pay taxes, for the authorities are ministers of God, attending to

[19] *Id.*
[20] *Id.*
[21] *Id.* at 176-178.
[22] *Id.* at 178-181.
[23] *Id.* at 181-184.
[24] *Id.* at 184-187.
[25] Wayne Grudem, *Business for the Glory of God: The Bible's Teaching on the Moral Goodness of Business* 69-70 (2003).

> this very thing.   Pay to all *what is owed* to
> them: taxes to whom taxes are *owed*, revenue to
> whom revenue is *owed*, respect to whom respect
> is *owed*, honor to whom honor is *owed*. *Owe* no
> one anything, except to love each other, for the
> one who loves another has fulfilled the law (Rom.
> 13: 6-8).

> As is evident in this translation, the command, "owe
> no one anything," is simply a summary of the obligations to
> pay what we owe as specified in the previous verses, whether
> taxes or respect or honor or so forth.   Therefore, if I have a
> mortgage on my house, I should make the mortgage
> payments when they are "owed"; that is, I should make
> payments on time as I have agreed to do. I do not "owe" the
> entire balance of the mortgage to the lender until the date
> specified. Though I have borrowed money and am carrying a
> long-term debt, I am completely obedient Romans 13:8, "owe
> no one anything," because I have no past-due payments on
> my mortgage.[26]

As the above makes clear, Dr. Grudem does not understand *Romans* 13:8
as being essentially limited to taxes, as Mr. Burkett does.   Rather, Dr.
Grudem understands *Romans* 13:8 to require one to pay debts and other
obligations as they become due—are *owed*. Dr. Grudem does not see
Romans 13:8, or any other passage, as forbidding borrowing and lending.
    Dr. Grudem, however, is not blind to the fact that borrowing carries
risks and in some cases may be unwise. After the discussion of *Romans*
13:8 set forth above, he notes:

> Of course, borrowing may at times be unwise (see Prov.
> 22: 7, "the borrower is the slave of the lender"; also Deut. 28:
> 12), and the ability to borrow may be misused by those who
> incur excessive debt (" The wicked borrows but does not pay
> back," Ps. 37: 21), and borrowing does carry some risk and
> some obligations that can be very hard to get out of (see Ex.
> 22: 14), but the Bible does not say that borrowing in itself is
> wrong.[27]

With that said, Dr. Grudem then turns to his arguments for the
fundamental goodness of borrowing and lending. He notes that borrowing

---

[26] *Id.* at 68-69 (emphasis in original).
[27] *Id.* at 69.

and lending multiplies "the usefulness of all the wealth in society."[28] He
begins by discussing examples such as borrowing and lending library
books and rental cars, both of which multiply the use of the items
borrowed and save the borrower from actually buying the items. This
multiplies the usefulness of the item (for it is as if many copies of the
library book, for example, as owned) while allowing the borrower to save
part of his wealth (that he did not have to spend to buy the item) for use
on other things.[29]

He then moves from a discussion of borrowing and lending of
physical objects to the borrowing and lending of money. He notes that it
essentially works the same way as with the physical objects, except that
money that is borrowed and lent multiplies many more times in society
given the unique nature of money.[30]

> The point is that if we could not borrow and lend
> money, but had to operate only on a cash basis, the world
> would have a vastly lower standard of living, not only in the
> richer nations but also in the poorer nations as well. The
> existence of borrowing and lending means that the total
> available amount of goods and services in the world has been
> multiplied many times over.
>
> In this way, borrowing and lending multiply
> phenomenally our God-given enjoyment of the material
> creation, and our potential for being thankful to God for all
> these things and glorifying him through our use of them.[31]

Dr. Grudem concludes by observing that there are of course many
temptations to sin with regard to borrowing and reminding the reader
that just because something can be perverted to evil doesn't make the
thing itself evil.[32] It isn't that Dr. Grudem thinks that unfettered
borrowing is a God-honoring way to live, or that he doesn't see any
dangers with regard to borrowing. Quite the contrary, as the following
quote demonstrates:

> As many Americans are now discovering, there is a great
> temptation to borrow more than is wise, or to borrow for
> things they can't afford and don't need, and thus they become
> foolishly entangled in interest payments that reflect poor
> stewardship and wastefulness, and that entrap people in a

---

[28] *Id.* at 70.
[29] *Id.* at 70-71.
[30] *Id.* at 72-73.
[31] *Id.* at 73.
[32] *Id.* at 73-74.

downward spiral of more and more debt. In addition, lenders can be greedy or selfish. Some lenders will lend to people who have no reasonable expectation of repaying and then take advantage of these people in their poverty and distress.[33]

Dr. Grudem is not unaware of the dangers of debt, he just sees more freedom with regard to borrowing that any of other three authors that we have considered in this chapter.

All four of the men discussed in this section are respected teachers of God's Word, and all four appear to love the Lord and desire to follow Him fully and to see others do so. Further, all four of these men have blessed me, and I have learned much from each of their ministries and would highly recommend their work to you. I obviously would not fully agree with any of the four of them on all issues, but that does not mean that I can't learn from them, even on issues where we disagree.

That said, I am not going to pick one of the above and tell you who is right. The reason for that is easy. I don't think I know who is right. This is an issue that, as of the writing of this book, I am still trying to decide exactly what I think the Scriptures require in this area. But, even without a definite answer, to consider these four positions, which seem to fit on a spectrum from most restrictive to least restrictive, is a very beneficial activity as we begin our study of debtor-creditor relations law.

Principles that We Can All Agree On

Regardless of the position one takes on the initial question of whether a Christian should borrow (whether you agree with Mr. Gothard, Dr. Rushdoony, Mr. Burkett, Dr. Grudem, or none of the four), there are certain principles that virtually every Christian can likely agree on with regard to debt. These principles are briefly discussed in the following.

First, whatever one borrows must be repaid. "The wicked borrows but does not pay back, but the righteous is generous and gives." *Psalm 37:21 (English Standard Version)*. The Bible does provide for debt forgiveness, which will be discussed in coming chapters. However, as an initial matter, it should be noted that whatever one borrows must be paid back.

Second, debt can be abused, become excessive, and feel like bondage; therefore, debt should generally be avoided except for certain limited situations. (Of course, as noted in the preceding, some would say all situations.) Borrowing to buy a home (or other asset that is likely to appreciate in value), to buy or start a business, to finance an education, on

---

[33] *Id.*

in a true emergency situation seems to be different in kind than borrowing for consumer reasons.

Third, short-term borrowing should generally be preferred over long-term borrowing. The longer one remains in a debt situation, the more risk one faces. As we will see in our study of debt forgiveness in the Bible, God seems to have a desire that His people be free of long-term debt as a general matter.[34] Further, as Dr. Burkett notes, long-term debt as it is understood today is a relatively new phenomenon. He writes:

> In an era of 30-and 40-year, and even longer, mortgages, avoiding long-term debt sounds almost impossible. But remember, such long-term debt is a relatively new idea. Our grandfathers, even many of our fathers, would have balked at loans that extended for three or four decades. They knew what this generation will eventually find out for themselves: If you stay in debt long enough, you will eventually get wiped out.[35]

Fourth, as a matter of wisdom, one should not sign as a surety or guarantor for another. *Proverbs* offers many warnings on the dangers of signing surety for another.[36] Even if this is not viewed as a command, it is clear that the Bible presents it as very unwise.

These four principles don't make any particular borrowing decision easy or obvious. However, it does provide us with at least a set of general principles from which we can reason, through prayer, Bible-study, and Godly counsel, to the particulars. God seems to have designed a world in which both legal and personal matters must be addressed in this fashion. It is not as easy or comfortable as bright-line rules, but it does keep us reaching for, searching after, and dependent upon the Lord God. Perhaps that is a part of the reason He made the world that way.

NOTES AND QUESTIONS

1. How much debt do you have? How much do you owe and to whom? Why did you borrow when you borrowed? Do you have a goal of being debt-free? Does your debt load cause you stress? What advice would you give to your parents, children, or friends about borrowing? Does it differ with age and season of life? If so, why? Does that tell us anything important about debt?

---

[34] *See, e.g., Deuteronomy* 15.
[35] Burkett, *supra* note 15, at 181.
[36] *See Proverbs* 6:1–5, 11:15, 17:18, 20:16, 22:26, and 27:13.

_____

_____

_____

_____

_____

_____

2. What do you think? Should Christians attempt to live debt-free? How would you answer the other questions raised in this chapter? If some debt is permissible, what kinds and how much? Is incurring debt a sin against God or is it just a wisdom issue? Should our modern debt systems be viewed as a blessing, much like viewing the concept of money as a good gift from God, or as a curse that is enslaving and impoverishing the nation? Is all of this debt a problem, or are we just making too much of it?

Do you find yourself agreeing more with Mr. Gothard, Dr. Rushdoony, Mr. Burkett, Dr. Grudem, or maybe none or some combination thereof? Why?

_____

_____

_____

_____

_____

_____

3. Other Christian Worldview Issues in the Debtor-Creditor Relations Setting. Obviously, as is hinted at in the preceding, there are other Christian worldview issues in the debtor-creditor relations law area. For example, the Bible does have some extensive regulations regarding lending and borrowing. Further, the Old Testament law presents a sophisticated system of debt relief. The following chapters will consider many of these issues.

CHAPTER 2
A LAW-OF-NATURE FRAMEWORK FOR ANALYZING COMMERCIAL LAW ISSUES

The primary goal of this book is to help you understand the law of debtor-creditor relations from a biblical worldview, or, to put it as those in the Founding era might have, to understand the law of nature and nature's God and how it governs the law of man in the area of debtor-creditor relations. This involves searching for general principles of law as found in the law of nature and nature's God and then attempting to apply those general principles to specific situations, both with regard to legislation made by legislators and common law principles and doctrines as discovered and applied by judges. The following excerpt discusses the "law-of-nature" approach in general and makes specific application to the topic of self-help repossession by a secured creditor.

Rodney D. Chrisman, *Can a Merchant Please God?: The Church's Historic Teaching on the Goodness of Just Commercial Activity as a Foundational Principle of Commercial Law Jurisprudence*
6 Liberty U. L. Rev. 453 (2012)[1]

[The first several parts of this article introduce the current absence of a consistent jurisprudential understanding of commercial law and discusses the progression of the church's teachings on commercial activity from generally viewing it favorably to viewing it unfavorably and back to

---

[1] Editor's Note: In the following article, many footnotes have been omitted, but others have been retained. For convenience sake, where they have been retained, there original numbering has not been retained. If you would like to see the entire article with all of the footnotes as they appear in the original, you may visit http://www.rodneychrisman.com/articles/ for a copy.

viewing it favorably. The article does this, primarily, by analyzing the *Opus imperfectum in Matthaeum* ("The Incomplete Work on Matthew") and the reinterpretation of its very anti-merchant teachings by the Scholastics.

The following excerpt picks up from there to argue that the biblical understanding that just commercial activity is a good thing can provide the foundational principle of commercial law jurisprudence. It uses self-help repossession to illustrate this point.]

V. Toward a Law-of-Nature Commercial Law Jurisprudence Based Upon the Foundational Principle that Just Commercial Activity is Pleasing to God

In another time, when people thought much differently, Justice Story of the United States Supreme Court could write of such a thing as "the general principles and doctrines of commercial jurisprudence" and general "principles of commercial law." [2] These general principles of commercial law where thought to be the same for all people for all time in all places:

> The law respecting [commercial activity] may be truly declared in the languages of Cicero, adopted by Lord Mansfield in *Luke* v. *Lyde*, 2 Burr. 883, 887, to be in a great measure, not the law of a single country only, but of the commercial world. *Non erit alia lex Romae, alia Athenis; alia nunc, alia posthac; sed et apud omnes gentes, et omni tempore una eademque lex obtinebit.*[3]

For centuries, courts in the West would reason from these general principles of commercial law to the particular facts of a given case. The departure from this way of thinking has greatly contributed to the current incomprehensibility of law and the related cynicism toward and contempt of law in the West. Given the disastrous results of this change in jurisprudential thinking, perhaps a return to early models and ways of thinking is in order.[4]

---

[2]. Swift v. Tyson, 41 U.S. 1, 18-19 (1842), *overruled by* Erie R. Co. v. Tompkins, 304 U.S. 64, 79-80 (1938).

[3]. *Id.* at 19. The quoted phrase from Cicero can be translated "nor will there be one law in Rome, another in Athens, another now, another in the future, but one law eternal and immutable will bind together all nations of all times." III MARCUS TULLIUS CICERO, DE RE PUBLICA 22 (James E.G. Zetzel) (1995).

[4]. Livy makes just such a suggestion in THE EARLY HISTORY OF ROME. He writes:
> I invite the reader's attention to much more serious consideration of the kind of lives our ancestors lived, of who were the men, and what the means both in politics and war by which Rome's power was first acquired and subsequently expanded; I would then have him trace the process of our moral decline, to watch,

Such a return should begin with the recognition that there are general principles of commercial law that are knowable and can serve as the basis for a jurisprudence of commercial law. Further, as the Scholastics eventually concluded, a foundational general principle of commercial law is that just commercial activity is a good thing.

On the first topic, i.e., that there are general principles of law that are knowable and can serve as a basis for legal analysis, there is perhaps no greater work than Dean Jeffrey Tuomala's magnificent article *Marbury v. Madison and the Foundation of Law*.[5] Of particular help for the topic at hand is Section IV of that article, which is captioned "*Marbury*—The General Principles of Law."[6] In that section of his article, Dean Tuomala asserts that "God's law not only provides the right to establish a framework of government, but it . . . . [A]lso provides other general principles of law."[7] It was with these other principles of law that the Scholastics were grappling when they reinterpreted the *Opus imperfectum*. These general principles formed the foundation for law for nearly a millennia in the West.

---

first, the sinking of the foundations of our morality as the old teaching was allowed to lapse, then the rapidly increasing disintegration, then the final collapse of the whole edifice, and the dark dawning of our modern day when we can neither endure our vices nor face the remedies needed to cure them. The study of history is the best medicine for a sick mind; for in history you have a record of the infinite variety of human experience plainly set out for all to see; and in that record you can find for yourself and your country both examples and warning; fine things to take as models, base things, rotten through and through, to avoid.

LIVY, THE EARLY HISTORY OF ROME 30 (Aubrey de Selincourt trans., Penguin Classics 2002). The prophet Jeremiah suggests a similar remedy for the people of Judah when he writes, "Thus says the Lord, 'Stand by the ways and see and ask for the ancients paths, Where the good way is, and walk in it; And you will find rest for your souls." *Jeremiah* 6:16. This is not a romantic imagining that the "the good old days" were much better. *Ecclesiastes* 7:10. Rather, it is an understanding that, when one's way has been lost, it is often helpful to return to the place in the road where the wrong turn was made.

5. Jeffrey Tuomala, Marbury v. Madison *and the Foundation of Law*, 4 LIBERTY U. L. REV. 297 (2010). Dean Tuomala does an outstanding job of describing (1) "law of nature" jurisprudence; (2) the historic character of law of nature jurisprudence, including its foundations in Christianity and God's law; (3) the departure from this way of thinking about the law; and (4) the related decent into a purely positivistic understanding of law, which has lead to the type of confusions throughout the law as are discussed particularly in this Article as they relate to commercial law. For the most part, this Article does not attempt to set out again all of Dean Tuomala's arguments, but rather the author commends the reader to Dean Tuomala's excellent article for a fuller explication of these important issues. That said, this Article generally accepts the premises and conclusions of Dean Tuomala's excellent work without additional examination, and it attempts to move on from there by attempting to understand and apply the "general principles of commercial law" in order to begin laying the foundation for a law of nature jurisprudence of commercial law. Further, throughout this Article, when a reference is made to a law-of-nature jurisprudential approach, it is intended to refer to the approach described and set out by Dean Tuomala in this article. *See, e.g., id.* at 315-16 & nn.95-98 (describing a law-of-nature jurisprudence and noting that it was "set out in the Declaration of Independence" and "is not simply a human convention").

6. *Id.* at 314-25.

7. *Id.* at 314-15.

In discussing these general principles and Chief Justice John Marshall's view of them, Dean Tuomala writes:

> He presupposed a preexisting law, whose source is identified in the Declaration of Independence, that grounds the right to establish a government, provides the general principles of law, and defines the nature of judicial power.
>
> Marshall's "general principles of law" may be identified in part with the "general principles of commercial law" to which Justice Story appealed in *Swift v. Tyson*. It is generally recognized that Story's opinion in *Swift* was grounded in law-of-nature jurisprudence. . . . *Swift* was based on the law-of-nature jurisprudence set out in the Declaration of Independence, that law is not simply a human convention. This jurisprudence provided the basic rule of law upon which thousands of decisions . . . were premised . . . .[8]

As noted earlier, however, the legal systems in the West have abandoned this way of understanding the law, and consequently "most contemporary lawyers, judges, and law professors do not recognize any law superior to the Constitution" which "means they will not recognize the existence of general principles of law as articulated in *Marbury* and *Swift*."[9]

Like Justices Holmes, Brandeis, and Frankfurter, among many others, they do not even believe that these principles exist. In the landmark case of *Eerie Railroad Co. v. Tompkins*, for example, Justice Brandeis, in overruling *Swift v. Tyson*, wrote that "[t]he fallacy underlying the rule declared in *Swift v. Tyson* is made clear by Mr. Justice Holmes. The doctrine rests upon the assumption that there is 'a transcendental body of law outside of any particular State but obligatory within it. . . . .'"[10] Further, in *Guaranty Trust Co. v. York*, "Justice Frankfurter . . . proclaimed that *Erie* had . . . actually established an entirely different way of looking at the law"[11] that did not include any higher general principles of law. Frankfurter too quoted Holmes, proclaiming that law should not be "conceived as a 'brooding omnipresence' of Reason" capable of providing general principles upon which law can be based.[12]

Without these general principles of law, most all areas of law, commercial law included, lack any foundation other than the will of the

---

8. *Id.* at 315-16 (footnotes omitted).

9. *Id.* at 316.

10. Erie R. R. Co. v. Tompkins, 304 U.S. 64, 79 (1938); *see also* Tuomala, *supra* note 5, at 323.

11. Tuomala, *supra* note 5, at 324.

12. Guaranty Trust Co. v. York, 326 U.S. 99, 102 (1945) (alluding to and quoting Justice Holmes's dissent in Southern Pacific Co. v. Jensen, 244 U.S. 205, 222 (1917), which stated that "[t]he common law is not a brooding omnipresence in the sky, but the articulate voice of some sovereign or quasi sovereign that can be identified"); *see also* Tuomala, *supra* note 5, at 324.

sovereign.[13] Being Realists and positivists, Justices Brandeis and Holmes would certainly agree, as is evidenced by Justice Brandeis's quote of Justice Holmes in *Erie*, which concludes that "'[t]he authority and only authority is the State, and if that be so, the voice adopted by the State as its own (whether it be of its Legislature or of its Supreme Court) should utter the last word.'"[14] As Dean Tuomala demonstrates, this led to a rejection of the centuries-old "foundational principle of Christian common law jurisprudence . . . that human will must be exercised in accord with right or reason to be law."[15] Not surprisingly, law based purely upon the will of the sovereign, or even law believed to be so based, appears to be arbitrary, meaningless, and without any substantial foundation. Also not surprisingly, it has not taken long for a strong cynicism to develop toward law and for law to be held in contempt by much of the people of the West.[16] Or, to put it another way as Professor Smith does in *Law's Quandary*, this shift in understanding the law has resulted in the reduction of the modern legal profession's "talk" about the law to little more than nonsense.[17] Accordingly, as stated at the beginning of this Article, commercial law lacks any coherent jurisprudence and there appears to be little hope of developing one any time soon, at least under the prevailing models of thought about the law.

Therefore, a return to the other model of thought about the law is warranted. Pursuant to that model of legal thought, such general principles of law really do exist, as evidenced by Justice Story's statements in *Swift v. Tyson* quoted earlier. Further, Christianity forms the basis for these general principles of commercial law. As Justice Story wrote elsewhere, "[t]here never has been a period, in which the common law did not recognize recognise Christianity as lying at its foundations."[18] In a similar vein, Dean Tuomala, writing of Justice Story's opinion in *Swift*, states that in *Swift* Justice Story

> cited opinions from multiple jurisdictions and different periods in history, not as evidence of some broader social

---

13. Tuomala, *supra* note 5, at 323-25.

14. *Id.* at 323 (quoting *Erie*, 304 U.S. at 79 (alteration in original) (quoting Black & White Taxicab & Transfer Co. v. Brown & Yellow Taxicab & Transfer Co., 276 U.S. 518, 535 (1928) (Holmes, J., dissenting)).

15. *Id.* at 324.

16. HAROLD J. BERMAN, LAW AND REVOLUTION: THE FORMATION OF THE WESTERN LEGAL TRADITION 40 (1983).

17. *See, e.g.*, STEPHEN D. SMITH, LAW'S QUANDARY 176-177 (2004).

18. Joseph Story, Address Discourse Pronounced upon the Inauguration of the Author, as Dane Professor of Law in Harvard University, August 25th, 1829, in THE LEGAL MIND IN AMERICA: FROM INDEPENDENCE TO THE CIVIL WAR 178 (Perry Miller ed., Cornell Univ. Press 1969) (1962) ("One of the beautiful boasts of our [United States] municipal jurisprudence is, that Christianity is part of the Common Law, from which it seeks the sanction of its rights, and by which it endeavours to regulate its doctrines . . . . There never has been a period in which the common law did not recognise Christianity as lying at its foundations.").

custom, but as evidence of what the law of God is on a particular matter of commercial law. The *Swift* opinion embodies the view that law is "permanent, uniform and universal." It does not change; it applies to everyone equally; and it applies in every part of the world. This was Blackstone's view of the common law, and it was also Lord Coke's view of the common law.[19]

In an important footnote, Dean Tuomala further elucidates this "permanent, uniform, and universal nature of the law to which Story alluded in *Swift*" by setting forth the entire context, from Cicero, of the Latin phrase quoted by Justice Story in *Swift*. It reads:

> [L]aw in the proper sense is right reason in harmony with nature. It is spread through the whole human community, unchanging and eternal, calling people to their duty by its commands and deterring them from wrong-doing by its prohibitions. When it addresses a good man, its commands and prohibitions are never in vain; but those same commands and prohibitions have no effect on the wicked. This law cannot be countermanded, nor can it be in any way amended, nor can it be totally rescinded. We cannot be exempted from this law by any decree of the Senate or the people; nor do we need anyone else to expound or explain it. *There will not be one such law in Rome and another in Athens, one now and another in the future, but all peoples at all time will be embraced by a single and eternal and unchangeable law*; and there will be, as it were, one lord and master of us all—the [G]od who is the author, proposer, and interpreter of that law.[20]

The Law of God provides the general principles of commercial law. It is only from these general principles of commercial law that one can hope to develop a consistent and coherent commercial law jurisprudence.

It is here, then, that the church's view of commercial activity becomes so very important. The church's historic view of commercial activity assists in determining the Law of God with regard to commercial activity and therefore the general principles of commercial law. Certainly,

---

[19]. Tuomala, *supra* note 5, at 318 (footnotes omitted); *see also* SMITH, *supra* note 17, 45-48 ("Blackstone and Story were, after all, heirs of a worldview that assumed that God was real—*more real* than anything else, in fact, or *necessarily* rather than just *contingently* real—and had created the universe according to a providential plan. This view had important implications for the nature of law.").

[20]. *Id.* at 318 n.106 (quoting Cicero, *The Republic, in* THE REPUBLIC AND THE LAWS 68-69 (Niall Rudd trans., 1998) (emphasis added)).

the church can be in error with regard to a particular teaching, as it was for some time when it concluded that commercial activity, and therefore merchants, could not please God.[21] As this Article demonstrated herein, however, the Scholastics moved the church away from this teaching, eventually concluding that just commercial activity is pleasing to God.[22] This teaching is consistent with the Bible.

The Bible assumes private property rights and a market economy.[23] Further, the Bible never condemns commercial activity in and of itself nor does it forbid Christians from becoming merchants.[24] The Bible does, however, have much to say about unjust commercial activity.[25] For example, it condemns unjust weights and measures,[26] forbids certain types of security interests that would be particularly harmful to the poor,[27] and demands respect for debtors in the repossession of collateral

---

[21]. Obviously, the author is a Protestant. Therefore, he adheres to *Sola Scriptura*—a Latin phrase from the Reformation that literally means "scripture alone" and summarizes the Reformation teaching "that Scripture alone is absolutely authoritative for doctrine and practice, and following Scripture alone is sufficient to please God in all things." THE ESV STUDY BIBLE 2614 (Wheaton, IL: Crossway Bibles, 2008). Popes, councils, the church fathers, and all other mortal men may err, but the Bible is infallible and is therefore the standard by which all things are to be judged. *See, e.g., Westminster Confession of Faith*, Chapter 1. For more on the differences between the Roman Catholic and Protestant approaches to law, *see* Jeffrey C. Tuomala, *Book Review: Robert George's* The Class of Orthoxies: Law, Religion, and Morality in Crisis, 3 LIBERTY U. L. REV. 77 (2009).

[22]. *See supra* Part IV [of this Article, which is available online at http://www.rodneychrisman.com/articles].

[23]. The command found in the Ten Commandments and elsewhere in the Bible not to steal makes sense only in light of private ownership rights in property. *See, e.g., Exodus* 20:15 and 22:1-4, *Leviticus* 19:11, *Deuteronomy* 5:19, *Proverbs* 30:9, *Matthew* 19:18, *Romans* 13:9, and *Ephesians* 4:28. Further, the commands against coveting the property of another imply the same thing. *See, e.g., Exodus* 20:17, *Deuteronomy* 5:21, *Matthew* 5:28, *Romans* 7:7 and 13:9, *Ephesians* 5:3-5, and *Colossians* 3:5; *see also* WAYNE GRUDEM, BUSINESS FOR THE GLORY OF GOD: THE BIBLE'S TEACHING ON THE MORAL GOODNESS OF BUSINESS 19-24 (2003) (discussing the goodness of ownership.)

Further, there are a number of passages in the Bible that condemn financial unfairness in the market, which of course assumes that there is such a thing as a market. *See, e.g., Leviticus* 19:35-36, *Deuteronomy* 25:13-15, *Proverbs* 11:1, 16:11, 20:10 and 23, *Micah* 6:11, and *Hosea* 12:7. Accordingly, the Bible implicitly affirms the free market by condemning those who act deceitfully in that market without condemning the market itself. *See also* GRUDEM, *supra* note 23, 61-66 (discussing the goodness of competition.)

[24]. In addition to the passages listed in the previous footnote, there are a number of craftsman and merchants in the New Testament who are never condemned for being merchants and are never commanded to seek out a different way of life. *See, e.g., Acts* 16:14-15, 40 (Lydia, who was a purple cloth merchant) and 18:2-3 (Aquila, Priscilla, and even the Apostle Paul, who were tentmakers.); *see also* GRUDEM, *supra* note 23, 35-45 (discussing the goodness of commercial transactions and profit).

[25]. *See, e.g., Leviticus* 19:35-36; *Deuteronomy* 25:13-15; *Proverbs* 11:1, 16:11, 20:10, 20:23; *Micah* 6:11; *Hosea* 12:7.

[26]. *Leviticus* 19:35-36; *Deuteronomy* 25:13-15; *Proverbs* 11:1, 16:11, 20:10, 20:23; *Micah* 6:11; *Hosea* 12:7.

[27]. *See Deuteronomy* 24:6 (forbidding the pledge of a handmill or upper millstone, which would leave the debtor without a way to grind grain for bread), 24:12-13 (requiring that a poor man's cloak, if taken in pledge, be returned to him at night so that he can sleep in it and be warmed), *Exodus* 22:25-27 (same), and *Deuteronomy* 24:17 (forbidding the pledge of a widow's garment).

that is located in a dwelling,[28] just to name a few. Taken together, these passages establish a foundational general principle of commercial law— that just commercial activity is pleasing to God and is a good thing.

This foundational principle would do much to begin unifying and organizing thought regarding commercial law. As an initial matter, it provides a deeper meaning to the oft-stated comment that "commercial law is merely the rules by which business people do their work." Commercial law is such a set of rules because it serves the interests of those engaged in commerce, but that is not all that it is. Instead, it provides the necessary legal framework to encourage just commercial activity and to discourage and punish unjust commercial activity. As noted here, this just commercial activity is pleasing to God and beneficial to society. Therefore, a legal framework that encouraged such activity, while taking adequate precautions against unjust practices, is a good thing and much more than just a collection of rules for the benefit of merchants.

For example, the law of secured transactions, a subset of commercial law, still provides for pledges and security interests, just as the law in the time of the Bible did.[29] Further, and still in accordance with the Law of God, it provides special rules for the repossession of collateral.[30] Article 9 of the Uniform Commercial Code provides that a secured creditor may repossess the collateral, often called self-help repossession, on the condition that this self-help repossession can be carried out without a breach of the peace.[31] Article 9, however, does not

---

[28]. *Deuteronomy* 24:10-11 (forbidding entrance into a debtor's house to take a pledge, requiring instead that the creditor remain outside and wait for the debtor to bring it out).

[29]. *Deuteronomy* 24:6 (forbidding the pledge of a handmill or upper millstone, which would leave the debtor without a way to grind grain for bread), 24:12-13 (requiring that a poor man's cloak, if taken in pledge, be returned to him at night so that he can sleep in it and be warmed), *Exodus* 22:25-27 (same), and *Deuteronomy* 24:17 (forbidding the pledge of a widow's garment); *see also* U.C.C. §§ 9-203(b)(3)(B), 9-207 & cmt. 2, 9-313 & cmt. 2 (2001); 4 JAMES J. WHITE & ROBERT S. SUMMERS, UNIFORM COMMERCIAL CODE: PRACTITIONER TREATISE SERIES 169 (6th ed. 2010) (identifying property that is properly "pledgeable").

[30]. *Deuteronomy* 24:6 (forbidding the pledge of a handmill or upper millstone, which would leave the debtor without a way to grind grain for bread), 24:12-13 (requiring that a poor man's cloak, if taken in pledge, be returned to him at night so that he can sleep in it and be warmed), *Exodus* 22:25-27 (same), and *Deuteronomy* 24:17 (forbidding the pledge of a widow's garment); *Deuteronomy* 24:10-11 (forbidding entrance into a debtor's house to take a pledge, requiring instead that the creditor remain outside and wait for the debtor to bring it out). It should be noted, however, that the acts referenced in these passages might be a reference solely to the initial taking of the collateral as a pledge. Nevertheless, the principles seem to carry forward such that if it applied to the initial taking, it appears that it would apply with equal force to all subsequent takings. For example, if you gave the poor man's cloak back to him at night after he failed to pay, and you come back the next day to take it and sell it, then it would in essence be a repossession and thus covered by these principles.

[31]. U.C.C. § 9-609 (2001).

supply a definition for what constitutes a breach of the peace.[32] Instead, it looks to the courts and the common law to provide such a definition.[33] Courts have generally concluded that a central concern in evaluating whether a breach of the peace has occurred is the risk of violence.[34] Further, courts have generally held that entering a dwelling without consent to retrieve collateral is per se a breach of the peace.[35] From a law-of-nature perspective, these two concerns within the context of breach of the peace can be easily explained and relate to issues much more important than just having a workable list of rules that clearly define how business people should conduct themselves. Both derive not merely from a set of rather arbitrary rules handed down by some particular sovereign but rather from the profound respect for human beings as being made in the image of God.[36]

Violence is a concern because people are made in the image of God, and therefore, violence against another human should only be carried out in situations where there is proper authority and justification for it. Self-help repossession, while furthering the laudable goal of encouraging just commercial activity, does not warrant physical violence. Rather, the secured party seeking repossession, when faced with the possibility of violence, must desist in its efforts to repossess, and instead it must petition the court in order to procure the assistance of the sheriff in repossessing the collateral.[37] While secured creditors do not have the

[32]. *See generally* U.C.C. art. 9 (2001); *see also* Deavers v. Standridge, 242 S.E.2d 331, 333 (Ga. Ct. App. 1978) (noting that the Uniform Commercial Code does not provide a precise definition of breach of the peace); U.C.C. § 9-609 cmt. 3 (stating that this particular section "does not define or explain the conduct that will constitute a breach of the peace, leaving that matter for continuing development by the courts").

[33]. U.C.C. § 9-609 cmt. 3 (2001).

[34]. *Deavers*, 242 S.E.2d at 333 (stating that a breach of the peace is usually indicated if there is "an accompanying incitement to immediate violence"); Morris v. First Nat'l Bank & Trust Co. of Ravenna, 254 N.E.2d 683, 686 (Ohio 1970) (noting that a breach of the peace is generally found when there is an incitement to violence); Harris Truck & Trailer Sales v. Foote, 436 S.W.2d 460, 464 (Tenn. Ct. App. 1968) (noting that the "breach of the peace there referred to must involve some violence, or at least threat of violence"); Salisbury Livestock Co. v. Colorado Cent. Credit Union, 793 P.2d 470, 474 (Wyo. 1990) (noting that one of the main factors for determining a breach of the peace is whether there is a "potential for immediate violence").

[35]. Laurel Coal Co. v. Walter E. Heller & Co., 539 F. Supp. 1006, 1007 (W.D. Pa. 1982) (noting that the "actual breaking of a lock or fastener securing property . . . constitutes a breach of the peace"); Riley State Bank of Riley v. Spillman, 750 P.2d 1024, 1030 (Kan. 1988) (stating that "forced entry into the debtor's premises would almost certainly be considered a breach of the peace . . . . [W]e view breaking and entering either the residence or business of a person a serious act detrimental to any concept of orderly conduct of human affairs and a breach of the peaceful solution to a dispute."); Berg. v. Wiley, 264 N.W.2d 145, 150 (Minn. 1978) (stating that even "non-violent, forcible entry to retake possession of a tenant's premises constitutes a breach of the peace"); *see also* WHITE & SUMMERS, *supra* note 151, at 442-50 (providing a detailed description of what courts have consistently found to constitute a breach of the peace).

[36]. *Genesis* 1:26-27, *Genesis* 9:5-6, *James* 3:9.

[37]. Marcus v. McCullom, 394 F.3d 813, 819 (10th Cir. 2004) (stating that repossession is only lawful if no breach of the peace occurs); Williams v. Ford Motor Credit Co., 674 F.2d 717, 719 (8th Cir. 19882) (affirming the principle that judicial process is required if a breach of the peace may

authority to use physical violence to retrieve collateral because they do not "bear the sword," the civil magistrate does have such authority.[38] Accordingly, the concern that there not be a breech of the peace, i.e., violence, in self-help repossession is grounded in a profound respect for human beings as being made in the image of God and the authority that God has entrusted to various institutions within society.[39]

Further, the respect for the dwelling of a debtor is also easily explained by reference to the general principles of commercial law. First, it should be obvious that entering a dwelling without consent greatly increases the risk of violence.[40] This undoubtedly helps to explain the principle that runs throughout the common law that "a man's home is his castle."[41] Such a principle is also related to the idea of biblical institutions and the proper jurisdiction of those institutions. The institution of the family has the proper and primary jurisdiction in the home, and this jurisdiction should be respected by others.[42]

In addition, the Bible specifically provides that a secured creditor may not enter a dwelling house to retrieve collateral.[43] Rather, the secured party must wait outside for the collateral to be brought out.[44] This would have been rather radical for the time, as it was typical in ancient times for creditors to plunder the goods and homes of debtors taking those things to which they took a fancy.[45] Again, this very specific

---

result from the repossession); *Laurel Coal Co.*, 539 F. Supp. at 1006 (noting that a creditor cannot proceed without judicial intervention if it can be done without a breach of the peace); Wade v. Ford Motor Credit Co., 668 P.2d 183, 189 (Kan. Ct. App. 1983) (noting that a person "proceeds at his own peril if he commit the slightest assault or other breach of the public peace"); *see also* WHITE & SUMMERS, *supra* note 151, at 443-50 (providing numerous examples of when creditors were required to seek assistance to avoid breaching the peace in their repossession efforts).

[38]. *Romans* 13:4; *see also* Roger Bern, *A Biblical Model for Analysis of Issues of Law and Public Policy: With Illustrative Applications to Contracts, Antitrust, Remedies, and Public Policy Issues*, 6 REGENT U. L. REV. 103, 116-124 (1995).

[39]. *Genesis* 1:26-27, *Genesis* 9:5-6, *James* 3:9; *see also* Bern, *supra* note 158, at 116-124.

[40]. *Marcus*, 394 F.3d at 819; *Williams*, 674 F.2d at 719; *Laurel Coal Co.*, 539 F. Supp. at 1006.

[41]. SIR EDWARD COKE, THE THIRD PART OF THE INSTITUTES ON THE LAWS OF ENGLAND 162 (1644) ("For a man's house is his castle, *et domus sua cuique est tutissimum refugium* [and each man's home is his safest refuge]; for where shall a man be safe, if it be not in his house.").

[42]. *See* Bern, *supra* note 38, at 119-20 & nn.84-85, 87 (establishing the jurisdictional propositions of the family and noting that one of man's duties is to respect the jurisdiction of his fellow man as being made in the image of God").

[43]. *Deuteronomy* 24:10-11 (forbidding entrance into a debtor's house to take a pledge, requiring instead that the creditor remain outside and wait for the debtor to bring it out).

[44]. *Id.*

[45]. 5 R. J. RUSHDOONY, COMMENTARIES ON THE PENTATEUCH: DEUTERONOMY 390-91 (2008).
> To protect men's houses and properties is to uphold God's order, because God has established the legitimate boundaries of the family's jurisdiction and freedom.
>
> A little thinking tells us what this law prevents when obeyed. When a money-lender can enter a house to choose his collateral, he can, with a practiced eye, inventory the contents of the house. It is then possible for him to urge the borrower to ask for more than he can repay. By this means, he can in time seize various valuable assets.

rule is based upon a profound respect for the individual debtor, who is also, despite his debts, made in the image of God. It is therefore inappropriate for the secured party to enter into the debtor's home, "his castle," to repossess the collateral. The secured party does not have the rightful jurisdiction to so do. Instead, the secured party must wait outside the house for the debtor to bring the collateral out.[46]

Using a law-of-nature approach, this brief example demonstrates that a coherent and consistent commercial law jurisprudence can be developed that is intellectually satisfying. It is so because it is grounded on more than merely the will of the sovereign, and it consists of more than merely just a set of rules governing what business people do. Instead, it looks for its force and validity to those general principles of law that govern all the earth and find their ultimate source in God.

NOTES AND QUESTIONS

1. What do you think? Are you convinced that the American legal system should return to its historic basis in the law of nature and nature's God? Can you think of other areas where the Law of God as found in the Bible speaks to commercial activity and debtor-creditor relations? (Don't worry if you can't, we will look at others as we move throughout the course.) If so, does the current legal system seem to line up with the Law of God or reject it for some other solution? What are some challenges that would be faced if the legal system attempted to align itself with the Law of God in areas where it now currently does not?

> For its own purposes, in various countries now, inventories of a man's house are required by the tax collector, or by the census bureau. By this means, the state knows more than it has a legitimate right to know, and it can plan to use that knowledge lawlessly.

Id. at 390.

[46]. Presumably, if the debtor refuses, the civil magistrate would have the authority to enter the house and retrieve the collateral. The Bible is silent as to this point, but that is not surprising. The Bible, like much ancient law, is paradigmatic in nature. 2 DOUGLAS K. STUART, THE NEW AMERICAN COMMENTARY – EXODUS 442-45 (E. Ray Clendenen et al. eds., 2006) (noting that "modern societies have generally opted for exhaustive law codes" but that "[a]ncient laws did not work this way."). Dr. Stuart pointed out that ancient law codes

> were paradigmatic, giving models of behaviors and models of prohibitions/punishments relative to those behaviors, but they made no attempt to be exhaustive. Ancient laws gave guiding principles, or samples, rather than complete descriptions of all things regulated. Ancient people were expected to be able to extrapolate from what the sampling of laws did say to the *general* behavior the laws in their totality pointed toward.

Id. Additionally, Dr. Stuart pointed out that "God's revealed covenant law to Israel was paradigmatic." *Id.; see also* Rodney D. Chrisman, *The Paradigmatic Nature of Biblical Law*, RODNEYCHRISMAN.COM (Aug. 11, 2010), http://www.rodneychrisman.com/2010/08/11/the-paradigmatic-nature-of-biblical-law/ (providing a more thorough discussion of the paradigmatic nature of ancient and biblical law).

Do you believe that just commercial activity is a good thing and therefore should be encouraged by the legal system? If so, how best does a legal system do that?

---

2. Should a Christian Sign Surety or Serve as a Guarantor?
As discussed in this chapter, a law-of-nature approach to question of commercial law requires that one look to the Law of God to determine what general principles exist there and then attempt to apply them to the legal system (and life choices of course.) To practice, let's try this question: "should a Christian sign surety or serve as a guarantor on a loan?"

To begin, we should consider what the Bible says with regard to surety/guaranty-type relationships. We should start with the Bible because it is the best source we have for determining the principles contained within the law of nature and nature's God. The Bible does speak to these types of relationships in a number of places. For example:

> [1] My son, if thou be surety for thy friend,
> *If* thou hast stricken thy hand with a stranger,
> [2] Thou art snared with the words of thy mouth,
> Thou art taken with the words of thy mouth.
> [3] Do this now, my son, and deliver thyself,
> When thou art come into the hand of thy friend;
> Go, humble thyself, and make sure thy friend.
> [4] Give not sleep to thine eyes,
> Nor slumber to thine eyelids.
> [5] Deliver thyself as a roe from the hand *of the hunter*,
> And as a bird from the hand of the fowler. [47]

We see from the above that the Bible strongly discourages such arrangements. Does that mean that they should not be a part of a legal system based upon the law of nature and nature's God? While it might be tempting to answer that question in the affirmative, deeper reflection will reveal that the Bible is not answering that question.

Rather, here, the Bible is instructing believers in wisdom. It is very unwise to enter into such an arrangement. However, that is different

---

[47] *Proverbs 6:1–5. See also Proverbs 11:15, 17:18, 20:16, 22:26, and 27:13.*

than saying such an arrangement should be illegal. In fact, the passage assumes that the arrangement is legal and enforceable, and that the person who has foolishly signed surety should not rest until he has managed to release himself from the arrangement because it is in fact legal and enforceable and could bring ruin on the person serving as a surety.

Compare this passage in provides to *Deuteronomy* 24:10-11 (forbidding the entering of a debtor's house to retrieve an item given in pledge.) Notice how the Bible reads very differently in these two passages. It would seem that a legal system based upon the Law of God would not prevent serving as surety, even though it is unwise,[48] but it would forbid secured creditors from entering debtors' houses without permission. Do you agree? Can you use this method to analyze other questions and issues?

———————————————————————————

———————————————————————————

———————————————————————————

———————————————————————————

———————————————————————————

———————————————————————————

---

[48] We live in a very paternalistic age. We have become used to the civil magistrate assuming a role very different from the one assigned the civil magistrate in the Bible (i.e., primarily that of punishing evildoers and praising that which is good.) We often now expect the civil magistrate to prevent all harm and loss; a role not assigned to it by God and one that, indeed, it cannot fulfill. We unfortunately look to the civil magistrate to make things that are unwise illegal so that people don't behave unwisely. The recent attempts to shrink the sizes of candy bars and sodas in order to prevent obesity is a fine example of such paternalistic attempts to keep people from making poor decisions. Such attempts are doomed to failure. There is a difference between something being merely unwise on the one hand and illegal (and therefore unwise) on the other. A legal system based upon the law of nature and nature's God must understand this distinction and endeavor to remain within its God-given role.

CHAPTER 3
A BIBLICAL ANALYSIS OF
SELF-HELP REPOSSESSION

In the previous chapter, we considered how to analyze questions that arise in debtor-creditor relations law pursuant to a law-of-nature jurisprudence. In this chapter, we will practice this skill again by considering the Christian worldview of self-help repossession.

One of the principal benefits of being a secured, as opposed to an unsecured, creditor is the right to self-help repossession. This right allows the secured creditor or its agent to "take possession of the collateral . . . without judicial process, if it proceeds without breach of the peace." Uniform Commercial Code § 9-609(a)(1) and (b)(2). In order to conduct a biblical analysis of the doctrine of self-help repossession, it is necessary to begin with the principles related to the topic found in the law of nature and nature's God. For that, look back to the previous chapter and considering again those portions of the excerpted article that relate to self-help repossession. Read the Scripture passages cited in the footnotes. Then, with the biblical principles in mind, consider the following case.

Salisbury Livestock Company v. Colorado Central Credit Union
793 P.2d 470 (Wyo. 1990)

GOLDEN, Justice.

This is an appeal from a directed verdict granted to appellees Colorado Central Credit Union, and Al Weltzheimer, Tom Clark, Gordon Srock, and Darren Boling, (all appellees will be referred to as Colorado Central in the analysis) in a trespass action resulting from a vehicle repossession that occurred on appellant Salisbury Livestock Company's lands. The district court granted the directed verdict after finding that Colorado Central's entry to conduct the repossession was privileged and that reasonable men could not differ on the verdict. We do not agree. We reverse the directed verdict and remand for a new trial.

FACTS

Salisbury Livestock Company (Salisbury Livestock) initiated the trespass action in response to Colorado Central's repossession of vehicles owned by George Salisbury III (young Salisbury) from Wyoming property of Salisbury Livestock. Salisbury Livestock is a family corporation run by young Salisbury's father, George Salisbury, Jr.; it is registered in Wyoming and possesses land in Wyoming and in Colorado. The disputed repossession of the vehicles took place on Salisbury Livestock's Ladder Ranch, which is on the Wyoming side of the Wyoming–Colorado state border.

Young Salisbury had pledged the repossessed vehicles, along with three others, as collateral for a $13,000 loan from Colorado Central in October of 1984. This loan was made while he was living in the Denver area. He defaulted on the loan in March, 1986. He had defaulted on the loan once before, in October of 1985, and Colorado Central had repossessed one of his vehicles, which he subsequently redeemed. Colorado Central had then given young Salisbury an extension until February 15, 1986, meaning that he paid only interest from October, 1985, until February, 1986. He made the February, 1986 payment, but did not make any further payments.

At some time in early 1986 young Salisbury left Denver and returned to Slater, Colorado, where he resided near the Salisbury Livestock Wyoming property on which his mother and father lived. Colorado Central sent notice of default to his Slater, Colorado mailing address in May, 1986, but did not receive a response. In July, 1986, Colorado Central decided to repossess the vehicles pledged as security on the loan. Weltzheimer, Colorado Central's credit manager, hired C.A.R.S.–U.S.A., a car repossession company to retrieve the vehicles.

On the evening of July 27, 1986, C.A.R.S.–U.S.A. owner Clark and employees Srock and Boling (and one other C.A.R.S.–U.S.A. employee not made a party to the action) left Denver with two tow trucks to repossess young Salisbury's vehicles. Before leaving Denver, Clark had called young Salisbury's Slater, Colorado home and received directions for finding it from an unidentified woman. The repossession crew arrived at young Salisbury's home about 5:00 the next morning. They found one of the vehicles, a van, parked just off the highway in front of the house and with the key in the ignition. Clark looked inside a small shed or garage on the property and scouted the area around the house for the other vehicles, but did not find them.

Taking the van, they drove a short distance back up the road they had just travelled, Colorado Highway 129, to a large "Salisbury" sign that had been mentioned as a landmark by the unidentified woman Clark talked to on the telephone, and which they had noticed on their way to young Salisbury's home. The sign was adjacent to a private drive or roadway. Although they could not see any vehicles from the highway, the repossession crew turned down the drive. After travelling about fifty yards they spotted several vehicles in the ranch yard. When they reached the vehicles they identified two from their assignment form, a Corvette and a conversion van. They pushed the Corvette onto the drive so that they could reach it with one tow truck, backed up to the conversion van with the other tow truck, hooked both vehicles up, and towed them away.

At the time, it was light, and appellees reported that they heard people stirring in a nearby building. They did not attempt to obtain permission to enter the property or to take the vehicles. Clark testified that he did not plan on contacting anyone as it was his intention to avoid a confrontation. George Salisbury, Jr. testified that after the repossession he discovered that the repossessors had apparently broken a two-by-four that was lying on the ground near the repossessed vehicles.

After the repossession young Salisbury explained his financial problems to his father. The two agreed on a loan that permitted young Salisbury to redeem the vehicles on August 4, 1986, with a check drafted by his father. Salisbury Livestock, owner of the Wyoming property from which the Corvette and conversion van were towed, then initiated this trespass action.

STANDARD OF REVIEW

We apply the same standard to review a directed verdict as was employed by the district court in deciding the motion for the directed verdict. That is, "we must, without weighing the credibility of the witnesses or otherwise considering the weight of the evidence, determine whether there can be but one conclusion as to the verdict that reasonable jurors could have reached." . . . In so doing, we consider the evidence in the light most favorable to the nonmoving party and give that party the benefit of all reasonable inferences from the evidence. We give no deference to the findings of the trial court.

ANALYSIS

Salisbury Livestock contends that the directed verdict was improper, as entry was without privilege under W.S. 34–21–962 (July

1986 Repl.) [1] (secured party's right to take possession after default) because an entry on lands of another without consent is a trespass, which is itself a breach of the peace. It argues that, if Restatement (Second) of Torts § 198 (1965) applies, the repossessors failed to make a demand for the vehicles, and that the time and manner of entry were otherwise unreasonable, so that the entry was not privileged. It disputes Colorado Central's assertion that it should be charged with knowledge of the loan to young Salisbury, and it claims that it is an innocent third party.

Colorado Central and the individual appellees respond that the trial court was correct that their entry was privileged by W.S. 34–21–962. They point specifically to the statute's second sentence, which states, "[i]n taking possession a secured party may proceed without judicial process if this can be done without a breach of the peace." Appellees claim that their entry to repossess the pledged vehicles was therefore privileged because they did not breach the peace. They further rely on the district court's finding that W.S. 34–21–962 is underlain by Restatement (Second) of Torts § 198. Finally, responding to Salisbury Livestock's assertion that the corporation is a third party not involved in the loan transaction between Colorado Central and young Salisbury, they point to young Salisbury's statement on his loan application that he was a part owner of Salisbury Livestock, which, they argue, means the corporation had constructive knowledge of the loan. The argument proceeds that, if Salisbury Livestock is charged with knowledge of the loan, then consent in the loan agreement provides another good defense to the trespass claim.

Our review convinces us that Salisbury Livestock is entitled to have a jury decide the merits of its argument. There is no real disagreement as to whether a trespass occurred.[2] The crux of this dispute is whether the entry to repossess was privileged either by the self-help statute or by consent. From our review of the evidence in a light favorable to Salisbury Livestock, we conclude that a reasonable jury could find that it was not.

In determining the application of our self-help statute, W.S. 34–21–962, there are three initial considerations. First, that statute is Wyoming's verbatim codification of [U.C.C. § 9-609. Section 9-609], in turn, incorporates the preexisting right of extrajudicial repossession. Comment, *Breach of Peace and Section 9–503 of the Uniform Commercial Code—A Modern Definition for an Ancient Restriction,* 82 Dickinson L.Rev.

---

[1] Editor's Note: This statute is the then in place Wyoming version of what is now U.C.C. § 9-609 cited in the introduction.

[2] A trespass against real property is simply defined as, "consist[ing] of an interference with the possessor's interest in excluding others from the land." Restatement (Second) of Torts § 163 (1965). In its ruling on the motion for a directed verdict the district court said, "I don't think that there's any doubt under any law that [the entry to repossess] was a trespass, because there was an intentional entering of the land of another."

351, 354 (1978). The drafters of the Uniform Commercial Code did not intend that [§ 9-609] create new rights or obligations concerning the self-help remedy. *Id.* In the same vein, this court has said before that we will not presume that a statute changes the common law unless it does so explicitly. The underlying common law governing this entry to repossess is expressed, as was recognized by the trial court, in Restatement (Second) Torts § 198.

Second, because the Wyoming statute is the enactment of a uniform law, our interpretation is governed by W.S. 8–1–103(a)(vii) (June 1989 Repl.): "Any uniform act shall be interpreted and construed to effectuate its general purpose to make uniform the laws of those states which enact it." Consequently, to make a consistent application in this case, we must consider what self-help acts our sister jurisdictions have found protected by the same, or similar, statutory language.

Finally, we agree with the statement that "courts disfavor self-help repossession because, if abused, it invades the legitimate conflict resolution function of the courts." Note, *Is Repossession Accompanied by Use of Stealth, Trickery or Fraud a Breach of the Peace Under Uniform Commercial Code Section 9–503?*, 40 Ohio St.L.J. 501, 504 (1979). While recognizing that W.S. 34–21–962 extends a conditional self-help privilege to secured parties, we will read the statute narrowly to reduce the risk to the public of extrajudicial conflict resolution. Although it is apparent that the self-help remedy is efficient for creditors and results in reduced costs of credit for debtors, *Id.* at 506, we must seek a reasonable balancing of that interest against private property interests and society's interest in tranquility.

We then look to the language of W.S. 34–21–962 to establish the parameters of the protection it offers to secured parties who seek to repossess collateral without judicial process. The statute provides in pertinent part that "[i]n taking possession a secured party may proceed without judicial process if this can be done without breach of the peace * * *." Obviously, the key to whether a self-help repossession is privileged by the statute is whether the peace has been breached. Colorado Central agrees, but argues that the facts demonstrate that there was no breach of the peace. Salisbury Livestock would have us define breach of the peace as including simple trespass.

W.S. 34–21–962 does not define breach of the peace, and there is no definition offered elsewhere in the Wyoming statutes that address rights of secured parties.[3] In our review of decisions from other jurisdictions we

---

[3] Wyoming's criminal breach of the peace statute, W.S. 6–6–102(a) (June 1988 Repl.), reads, "[a] person commits breach of the peace if he disturbs the peace of a community or its inhabitants by using threatening, abusive or obscene language or violent actions with knowledge or probable cause to believe he will disturb the peace." Restatement (Second) of Torts § 116 is more useful in arriving at what constitutes a civil

find no consistently applied definition, but agree with the analysis of the Utah Supreme Court in *Cottam v. Heppner,* 777 P.2d 468, 472 (Utah 1989), that, "[c]ourts have struggled in determining when a creditor's trespass onto a debtor's property rises to the level of a breach of the peace. The two primary factors considered in making this determination are the potential for immediate violence and the nature of the premises intruded upon." These factors are interrelated in that the potential for violence increases as the creditor's trespass comes closer to a dwelling,[4] and we will focus our analysis on them. It is necessary to evaluate the facts of each case to determine whether a breach of the peace has occurred.

We agree with the trial court that the Restatement (Second) of Torts § 198 reasonableness requirement provides appropriate criteria for evaluating whether a creditor's entry has breached the peace. If, as here, there was no confrontation and the timing and manner, including notice or lack of notice, are found reasonable, the entry is privileged. If the jury should find that the manner or timing of this entry was unreasonable because it may have triggered a breach of the peace, it in effect finds the entry a breach of the peace and unprivileged. We foresee the possibility that a rational jury could reach the conclusion that this entry was unreasonable.

As asserted by Salisbury Livestock, one specific inquiry is whether, as discussed in Comment d, § 198, a demand for the property is required. The comment waives the requirement if such demand would be futile, but there must be a determination whether demand would have been futile in these circumstances. Young Salisbury had not responded to Colorado Central's demands for payment, but Salisbury Livestock, on whose property the vehicles were found, was not given an opportunity to deliver the pledged vehicles to Colorado Central or its representatives. Notice is not an express requirement of the statute, but is a common law element which helps to determine the reasonableness of the repossessors' actions. Because we recognize that there was no intent to alter the common law of repossession with W.S. 34–21–962, we believe the Utah Supreme Court's discussion of the § 198 notice requirement in *Mortensen v. LeFevre,* 674 P.2d 134 (1983) is applicable. Although that case did not involve a repossession, it did involve the § 198 "Privileges Arising Irrespective of Any Transaction Between the Parties," which is the situation with repossession from third party property.

---

breach of the peace: "A breach of the peace is a public offense done by violence, or one causing or likely to cause an immediate disturbance of public order." We note that, although actual violence is not required to find a breach of the peace, a disturbance or violence must be reasonably likely, and not merely a remote possibility.

[4] Decisions elsewhere have established a general rule that a creditor's entry into a residence without permission is a breach of the peace. J. White & R. Summers, *Handbook of the Law Under the Uniform Commercial Code* 26–6 (2d ed. 1980).

Neither of the *Cottam* factors, nor the Restatement reasonableness analysis, requires or suggests that a trespass is necessarily a breach of the peace. Property owners may be entirely unaware of a trespass, so that there is no potential for immediate violence. Likewise, a peaceful, inadvertent trespass on lands remote from any home or improvements is unlikely to provoke violence. Therefore, we do not agree with Salisbury Livestock's contention that a trespass without more is a breach of the peace. A trespass breaches the peace only if certain types of premises are invaded, or immediate violence is likely.

However, we cannot agree with Colorado Central's assertion that there can be no finding of a breach of the peace because there was no confrontation. Confrontation or violence is not necessary to finding a breach of the peace. Two elements of this case create questions which we believe might lead reasonable jurors to a conclusion at odds with the trial court's directed verdict. First, this was an entry onto the premises of a third party not privy to the loan agreement. Particularly if there was no knowledge of young Salisbury's consent to repossession, this could trigger a breach of the peace. The few reported cases involving repossession from third party properties suggest that such entry is acceptable. However, these cases do not address third party residential property. When entry onto third party property is coupled with the second unusual element, the location and the setting of this repossession, the possibility of a different verdict becomes more apparent.

We have not located any cases addressing a creditor's entry into the secluded ranchyard of an isolated ranch where the vehicles sought are not even visible from a public place. The few cases involve urban or suburban driveways, urban parking lots, or business premises. We believe that the location and setting of this entry to repossess is sufficiently distinct, and the privacy expectations of rural residents sufficiently different, that a jury should weigh the reasonableness of this entry, or whether the peace may have been breached by a real possibility of imminent violence, or even by mere entry into these premises: the area next to the residence in a secluded ranchyard.

Because these are factual questions on which reasonable minds may differ, it was error to grant the motion for a directed verdict. The jury must determine whether the peace was breached by this creditor's entry because of the premises entered or the real possibility of immediate violence given the setting and location of the repossession. The reasonableness of the time and manner of the entry must be considered in the context of the third party property status and the rural setting. Whether notice is necessary is also an appropriate consideration when evaluating the manner of repossession. If either time or manner, or both, are found unreasonable then the entry is not privileged.

The jury may also consider whether Salisbury Livestock had constructive knowledge of young Salisbury's consent to repossession because of his ownership interest in the corporation and the statements he made concerning his interest on the loan application. If Salisbury Livestock is charged with constructive knowledge of the consent, that knowledge privileges the entry to repossess against a claim of trespass. Consent of the possessor or another authorized to consent is an absolute defense to trespass.

We are sensitive to the usefulness of self-help remedies for secured parties, and recognize that W.S. 34–21–962 authorizes secured parties to proceed by action if self-help will not result in a breach of the peace. However, we must balance this concern with our recognition of society's interest in tranquility, and the right of those not involved with the security agreement to be free from unwanted invasions of their land, which trespass law generally protects against. To achieve an equitable balance where there is conflict, the finder of fact must weigh the particular facts and determine whether the repossession was conducted reasonably.

* * *

Reversed and remanded for a new trial.

CARDINE, Chief Justice, dissenting.

I would affirm. The court in this opinion notes that the few reported cases in point would find this entry of directed verdict "acceptable." So would I.

Appellant seeks to recover damage because appellees' agent, while driving on appellant's gravel road, broke a 2 x 4 board. Thereafter, without a breach of the peace, appellees took possession of cars that they were entitled to possess. This they were privileged to do pursuant to W.S. 34–21–962, which provides: "In taking possession a secured party may proceed without judicial process if this can be done without breach of the peace * * *."

Undertaking to repossess these cars under the circumstances here existing may have been risky, but that is often the case with repossession by exercise of self help. It is not uncommon for the secured creditor to take possession of property from the debtor or from his presence without judicial process. If taking possession can be accomplished without a breach of the peace, it is entirely lawful.

The secured party in this case, Colorado Central Credit Union, took possession without a breach of the peace. This was lawful, and the judgment should be affirmed.

NOTES AND QUESTIONS

1. What do you think? How would you have ruled in the above case? How would your analysis or the result reached be different, if at all, if you had of applied the biblical principles related to self-help repossession previously stated?

_____

_____

_____

_____

_____

2. Is Self-Help Repossession Consistent with Biblical Teachings at all? An argument can be made that self-help repossession is not consistent with biblical principles at all and therefore should be abolished. Certainly it works to encourage debtors to pay what they owe, which is consistent with the Bible. *See, e.g., Pslam* 37:21 (asserting that the wicked borrow and do not repay). Debtors have a biblical duty to keep their word and repay what they owe, and the law should encourage debtors to do that.

Self-help repossession likely does do this in at least two ways. First, and most obviously, once a creditor has repossessed a piece of collateral, the creditor is permitted by Article 9 of the U.C.C. to sell it in a commercially reasonable manner and apply the monies received to the balance of the debt owed. Accordingly, the debtor is forced through self-help repossession to submit the sale of the collateral in order to provide at least some payment to the secured party.

Second, self-help repossession has a sort of *in terrorem* effect that probably encourages many debtors to strive mightily to repay a secured loan. Car loans would be the primary example here. The thought that a car could be repossessed in the dead of night or while one is at work or some other unexpected time creates a good deal of angst in the debtor's mind that will often encourage greater efforts toward repayment.

However, there are other biblical principles that argue against self-help repossession. For example, until the secured party has rightly exercised sufficient dominion and control over the collateral, it is still the debtor's property. The Bible has a high view of property rights.

Further, even if there is no breach of the peace and the repossessor really attempts to avoid any such breach, there is still a risk of violence any time two private persons attempt a nonconsensual transfer of property. Normally, a nonconsensual transfer of property is called theft, and, for obvious reasons, including both respect for the image of God in a person and respect for private property rights, is condemned by the law. Self-help repossession is an exception, but that does not mean that it is not a risky one, as the dissent in the above case notes.

In addition, it does not respect the various jurisdictions or forms of government created by God. Of all the forms of government, only the civil magistrate is entrusted with the use of physical force in order to coerce one to obey the law. Private individuals may engage in self-defense, etc., but they may not use force on their neighbors in order to cause them to obey the law. Self-help repossession is, again, recognized as an exception to the general principle. However, there appears to be no biblical warrant for such an exception, and the principles described above, in addition to the fact that God has given the powers of the sword to the civil magistrate and not other forms of government, would seem to argue that this exception is unjustified.

Lastly, research indicates that it is not as effective in encouraging just commercial activity, i.e., repayment of debts, as one might first imagine. Where it has been eliminated, it has lead to an imperceptible rise in interest rates on car loans. Apparently, the remedies available through judicial process are sufficiently close in value to self-help repossession that lenders don't really charge all that much to forgo the right. This would seem to indicate that just commercial activity is not impeded, or at least not impeded much, by the removal of this right.

All of that said, what do you think? Is self-help repossession consistent with the Bible? Should it be kept, eliminated, or in some way modified? If you were in your state's legislature, what would you propose?

_____

_____

_____

_____

_____

CHAPTER 4
IS BANKRUPTCY BIBLICAL?

Not surprisingly, Christians get in financial troubles, and therefore may find themselves considering bankruptcy, just like unbelievers do. Just because the Lord God has regenerated someone does not mean that he is now immune from sin or hardships. The biggest difference is (or certainly should be) that, while an unbeliever likely will not care, a believer will often want to know what God thinks about filing bankruptcy. The believer is (or, again, should be) concerned with whether bankruptcy is biblical.

Similarly, a Christian legal professional may end up working in the area of debtor-creditor relations law, politics, or some other area touching on bankruptcy law. Further, all Christians have a duty to vote, and all Christians should be concerned as to whether we have just laws that are in accordance with God's law. Therefore, all Christians, whether in financial trouble or not, should be concerned with the question: "is bankruptcy biblical?"

As a Christian legal professional whose career has centered around business, tax, and commercial law, I have often had believers come to me in times of financial strain inquiring about bankruptcy. Usually, they want to know something of the procedure and process of bankruptcy, how long it will take, and what the results and consequences will be. Further, they are almost always concerned about whether it is a sin to file bankruptcy. In the following, I share what I have told them over the years, and I hope that it will be helpful to you in both advising those considering bankruptcy and in evaluating what a just bankruptcy system would be like (and therefore getting closer to understanding what our bankruptcy system should be like in order to honor the Lord.)

The Wicked Borrows but does not Repay

Psalm 37:21 is a good place to start in considering whether a Christian should file bankruptcy. It states "[t]he wicked borroweth, and payeth not again: [b]ut the righteous sheweth mercy, and giveth." Incurring a debt is the making of a promise—i.e., the promise to repay, and God's Word demands that promises be kept. *See, e.g., Exodus* 20:16, *Leviticus* 19:11, *Psalm* 15:1-4 and 58:3, *Proverbs* 6:16-19, *Ecclesiastes* 5:4-7, *Matthew* 5:33-37, *Ephesians* 4:25, and *Colossians* 3:9. Accordingly, the Christian considering bankruptcy is immediately faced with a dilemma— the Bible clearly teaches that borrowing and failing to repay is a sin and bankruptcy allows one to do just that.

Before moving to consider the Bible's system of debt relief and thereby attempting to resolve this dilemma, it is good to consider the Bible's command to keep one's word by repaying and its implications in this setting. We should always begin the analysis of any situation in life by asking what God has commanded of us. We should not begin by asking what God has commanded of others and attempt to hold them to that.

We must stand before God in judgment alone, and it is no answer to say, "I would have obeyed fully if everyone else around me would just act right." This is blame shifting, and it was one of the first consequences of the original sin in the garden—they recognized they were naked, they hid from God, and immediately upon being confronted with their sins they starting trying to blame shift. In this regard, we will fair no better than our original parents did. God sees through blame shifting and is not impressed by it. An obedient and responsible Christian should not start by blaming others or circumstances. An obedient and responsible Christian should want to begin by repenting and believing God for forgiveness, mercy, and grace.

Accordingly, the place to begin to answer this question is by noting that borrowing and not repaying is sin for which repentance is required. While it may be possible to get into financial distress where bankruptcy becomes a real possibility without sinning (say, for instance, if a person who has otherwise been perfectly financially responsible incurs a debilitating and expensive medical condition which costs him his job and causes him to incur medical bills that he cannot pay in order to stay alive,) in my experience, most people in financial distress did not get there without sin. They generally have incurred too much debt and spent too recklessly. To put it another way, they have not been good stewards with what God has entrusted to them. (And, I have experienced this first hand. I have not filed bankruptcy or failed to repay a creditor, but I have, at times, been a very poor steward of the financial resources with which God has entrusted me—incurring too much debt and spending recklessly.) Thus, they should begin with genuine repentance.

To put it another way, our disobedience (or our situation, even if not arrived at through disobedience) does not give us a claim on the grace and mercy of others. Mercy and grace to which one has a claim is by definition something other than mercy and grace. Our disobedience does not give us a claim on the obedience of others. Rather, our disobedience should lead us to repent, believe, and obey. It should cause us to be willing to entrust ourselves into the hands of God and suffer any consequences in a way that would honor Him. It should not make us think that we can demand grace, mercy, and obedience from other people. The issue of their obedience is between them and God. This is true in the realm of finances just as it is in virtually all of life.[1]

This is true notwithstanding the fact that the Bible commands lenders to be gracious, treating others as they would want to be treated themselves in a similar situation. God often imposes duties on both sides of a transaction or situation, and those duties are not dependent upon the other side fulfilling their duties. God commands wives to respect their husbands and husbands to love their wives, but neither commandment is dependent upon the other being fulfilled before it becomes effective. No husband can say, and honor God, "I will love you as soon as you finally start respecting me." God says love your wife. Period. It is not a contingent duty. Similarly, debtors may not say to creditors, "you have a duty to be gracious to me and to treat me like I want to be treated—therefore, you must forgive my debt." Debtors should begin with their own duties to God and to others, and, in this area, it is clear that the foundational duty is to repay what you have borrowed.

---

[1] The only possible exceptions to this lie in situations like the family. Obviously, I, as a father, am in a position to demand the obedience of my children. I can command them to, for instance, forgive a brother or sister who has wronged them, particularly when they are younger and therefore more subject to my commands. Even if I have wronged one of them, I can demand and exhort them to obedience, which would include forgiving me because God commands us to be forgiving. However, I should never attempt to demand their obedience before my own. Thus, I should first repent to God and to them fully admitting my sin and attempting to make whatever restitution is available to me (which, in many cases, will only be an honest and contrite apology.) Then, I should fulfill my God-given role as father and exhort them to their biblical duties. That said, in my experience, children are quick to forgive in these situations and need little exhortation.

All of that said, the situation of father (or mother) and child has little application to the debtor-creditor situation. Rarely will the one who incurred the debt be in a position of authority and discipleship *over* the creditor to whom the debt is owed. Therefore, it is quite safe to say that the place for the vast majority of debtors to begin is with their responsibility before God to repay what they owe quite apart from whatever duties God might place on creditors.

Therefore, in considering the issue of whether a Christian should file bankruptcy and in considering whether a legal system should include a system of bankruptcy, the starting point is a recognition that debts should be repaid. For a Christian considering bankruptcy, this will often mean repentance and financial counseling to make sure that the pattern that lead to the consideration of bankruptcy is not repeated. For a legal system that desires to be in accord with God's law, this means first making sure that the legal system has a robust and effective system for the enforcement and collection of legally owed debts. Once that is in place, then an institution of some system for debt relief is appropriate.

The Biblical System of Debt Relief

While it is often surprising to those who have not read the Old Testament law, the Bible contains a robust system of debt collection and relief. The Bible's system of debt collection, at least in parts, is considered in other areas of this book. This chapter is dedicated, again, at least in part, to a consideration of the Bible's system of debt relief. For such a consideration, the best place to begin is *Deuteronomy* 15:1-18.

> **15** At the end of *every* seven years thou shalt make a release. ² And this *is* the manner of the release: Every creditor that lendeth *ought* unto his neighbour shall release *it*; he shall not exact *it* of his neighbour, or of his brother; because it is called the Lord's release. ³ Of a foreigner thou mayest exact *it again*: but *that* which is thine with thy brother thine hand shall release; ⁴ Save when there shall be no poor among you; for the Lord shall greatly bless thee in the land which the Lord thy God giveth thee *for* an inheritance to possess it: ⁵ Only if thou carefully hearken unto the voice of the Lord thy God, to observe to do all these commandments which I command thee this day. ⁶ For the Lord thy God blesseth thee, as he promised thee: and thou shalt lend unto many nations, but thou shalt not borrow; and thou shalt reign over many nations, but they shall not reign over thee. ⁷ If there be among you a poor man of one of thy brethren within any of thy gates in thy land which the Lord thy God giveth thee, thou shalt not harden thine heart, nor shut thine hand from thy poor brother: ⁸ But thou shalt open thine hand wide unto him, and shalt surely lend him sufficient for his need, *in that* which he wanteth. ⁹ Beware that there be not a thought in thy wicked heart, saying, The seventh year, the year of release, is at hand; and thine eye be evil against thy poor brother, and thou givest him nought;

and he cry unto the Lord against thee, and it be sin unto thee.
[10] Thou shalt surely give him, and thine heart shall not be grieved when thou givest unto him: because that for this thing the Lord thy God shall bless thee in all thy works, and in all that thou puttest thine hand unto. [11] For the poor shall never cease out of the land: therefore I command thee, saying, Thou shalt open thine hand wide unto thy brother, to thy poor, and to thy needy, in thy land.

[12] *And* if thy brother, an Hebrew man, or an Hebrew woman, be sold unto thee, and serve thee six years; then in the seventh year thou shalt let him go free from thee. [13] And when thou sendest him out free from thee, thou shalt not let him go away empty: [14] Thou shalt furnish him liberally out of thy flock, and out of thy floor, and out of thy winepress: *of that* wherewith the Lord thy God hath blessed thee thou shalt give unto him. [15] And thou shalt remember that thou wast a bondman in the land of Egypt, and the Lord thy God redeemed thee: therefore I command thee this thing to day. [16] And it shall be, if he say unto thee, I will not go away from thee; because he loveth thee and thine house, because he is well with thee; [17] Then thou shalt take an aul, and thrust *it* through his ear unto the door, and he shall be thy servant for ever. And also unto thy maidservant thou shalt do likewise. [18] It shall not seem hard unto thee, when thou sendest him away free from thee; for he hath been worth a double hired servant *to thee*, in serving thee six years: and the Lord thy God shall bless thee in all that thou doest.

There is far too much in this passage for a thorough exegesis here. However, some issues regarding debt relief come immediately into view from this passage. First, debt relief in the Old Testament law is tied to the idea of the Sabbath Year. The Sabbath Year occurred every seventh year. Just as the seventh day was a day of rest to be kept holy, the Sabbath Year was a year of rest, also to be kept holy. As a part of the Sabbath Year, there is a forgiveness of debt and a manumission (or freeing) or bondservants or slaves.

Second, the debt relief in the Old Testament law was a universal grant of relief. It did not exclude any debt and it was not conditioned upon how the debt was incurred. The only limitation is with regard to membership within God's covenant people—those within the nation of Israel. Those outside the covenant were not entitled to debt relief and manumission. For those within the covenant, the debt relief and manumission described here appears to be absolute. Presumably, this and other benefits of being a part of God's people would have enticed others to want to join God's covenant people and to take note of the wonderful laws that God has given His people.

This is remarkable for its demonstration of mercy and grace to all of the citizens of Israel, regardless of their wealth and social standing, and regardless of how the particular debt or debts in question were incurred. As R. J. Rushdoony points out, there were essentially two ways that one could fall into debt or, even more severely, bondservice: incurring a debt and being unable to pay it or being required to make restitution for theft. "A man could be sentenced to bondservice to make restitution for an unpaid debt, or for theft."[2]

Accordingly, this law provided debt relief not only for the typical situation where a debt had been incurred in the general course of life and the debtor is unable to repay but also where the debt had been incurred through malfeasance of the debtor. A simple example from a passage of the Old Testament law dealing with theft will suffice to illustrate the point. Exodus 22 provides that "[i]f a man shall steal an ox, or a sheep, and kill it, or sell it; he shall restore five oxen for an ox, and four sheep for a sheep. . . . [H]e should make full restitution; if he have nothing, then he shall be sold for his theft."[3] There is an amazing demonstration of God's grace in the fact that even though he incurred his debt, which he could not repay which resulted in his being sold, he should still experience debt relief and go free of his bondservice in the seventh year.[4]

It is not entirely clear whether the manumission of bondservants is in the Sabbath Year or after six years of service regardless of when the Sabbath Year falls. Commentators appear to struggle with this question. Dr. Rushdoony states simply that "[a] release was necessary on the Sabbath or seventh year."[5] The *ESV Study Bible* states that "[t]he sabbatical year provides a limit to such slavery (cf. Ex. 21:2–6; Lev. 25:39–46)."[6] The *New American Commentary: Deuteronomy* asserts that the debtor-bondservant would serve "until either he had paid off his obligations or served for a six-year period (v. 12). Thereupon he was to be released from his economic bondage so that once again he could be free and independent."[7] Comparing *Deuteronomy* 15 with *Exodus* 21 and *Leviticus* 25, a somewhat complicated and nuanced system appears to result, the explication of which is beyond the scope of this chapter. Suffice

---

[2] Rousas John Rushdoony, Commentaries on the Pentateuch: Deuteronomy 233 (2008).

[3] *Exodus* 22:1-4.

[4] It is not entirely clear whether the release here is in the Sabbath Year or after six years of service regardless of when the Sabbath Year falls. Commentators appear divided on the point.

[5] Rushdoony, Commentaries *supra* note 2, 234.

[6] The ESV Study Bible 354 (2008).

[7] Eugene H. Merrill, The New American Commentary (Volume 4): Deuteronomy 245–246 (1994) (footnote omitted).

it to say for our purposes here, that, regardless of how the debt was incurred, bondservice for a period of no more than six years was required.

In summary, the Bible clearly provides a just and gracious system of society-wide debt relief. Normal debts were relieved in the Sabbath Year, which occurred every six years. Therefore, no debt would exceed six years in duration. Further, as a remedy for the collection and enforcement of debts, a debtor unable to pay his debt could be sold into bondservice. Regardless of whether the debt was incurred innocently or through malfeasance, the debtor-bondservant would serve no more than six years. He would then go free from both his debt and the related bondservice. As the system of debt relief demonstrates, God's law is manifestly both just and gracious.

Comparing the U.S. System of Debt Relief with the Biblical System

Since the Bible provides for a system of debt relief, then filing for bankruptcy is not per se a sin. Further, it would seem that a just legal system should include a system of debt relief since the biblical system does. Therefore, a Christian can file for bankruptcy without sin. The issue will then be a comparison of the United States bankruptcy system with the system of debt relief found in the Bible.

An exhaustive comparison of this type is beyond the scope of this chapter. However, it is useful to note a couple of differences by way of example. The examples should give some type of framework for a Christian who is considering bankruptcy to use, in conjunction with his local church, to evaluate if and how he should proceed through the bankruptcy process.

Obviously, the United States bankruptcy system bears some similarities to the biblical system. For example, both clearly contemplate debt relief, and both seem to be based in part on the idea that people should be given a second chance and a fresh start. However, that being said, there are some significant differences. A couple of these are discussed below.

First, the biblical system of debt relief is society wide, and it is centered primarily around the Sabbath year. The U.S. system, on the other hand, is primarily debtor initiated.[8] This does present some significant issues that should be considered in comparing the systems. For example, creditors in the U.S. system will find planning more difficult than creditors under the biblical system because U.S. debt relief is not automatically triggered upon set intervals, but rather is triggered by the debtor deciding to file a voluntary petition for bankruptcy. Creditors can

---

[8] Debtors can also be "forced" into bankruptcy by the filing of an involuntary petition. However, these are quite rare and the vast majority of bankruptcies begin by the filing of a voluntary petition by the debtor.

perhaps predict with some certainty how many debtors will file bankruptcy, etc., out of a given set of loans, but this is a far cry from the certainty of an every seventh year system as contemplated by the Bible.

Second, as you will learn in your studies, there are many debts that are not dischargeable in the U.S. system. Debts related to fraud and other malfeasance are not dischargeable, nor are student loan debts. The biblical system on the other hand appears to discharge all debts, regardless of how they are incurred. A debt incurred for fraud would appears to be dischargeable just as a debt incurred more innocently.

All Christians should be concerned as to how these and other differences might indicate changes that need to be made in the U.S. system to bring it in line with the biblical ideal. Further, Christians contemplating bankruptcy, with the help of their churches and church leaders, should consider how these differences might impact how and if a Christian should proceed through the bankruptcy system. Finally, Christian legal professionals working in the area of debtor-creditor relations law should be particular award of the similarities and differences between the U.S. and biblical system of debt relief so that they can advocate for change where needed and properly advise Christian and other clients seeking debt relief.

Notes and Questions

1. What would you do? Do you prefer our system or debt relief or the Bible's? Do you find the Bible's system of debt relief to be both just and gracious? If you were crafting a system of debt relief for modern society based upon the Bible, what would it look like?

_____

_____

_____

_____

_____

2. What would you tell him? If a friend of yours came to ask you whether he should file bankruptcy, what would you tell him?

_____

_____

_____

_____

_____

3. Reforming the Bankruptcy Code? If you were a member of Congress, would you suggest reforms to the Bankruptcy Code based upon the biblical system of debt relief? If so, what would they be? (As you progress through your studies of American bankruptcy law, keep these questions in mind.)

_____

_____

_____

_____

_____

CHAPTER 5
THE PURPOSES OF BANKRUPTCY

Charles J. Tabb and Jillian K. McClelland, Living with the Means Test
31 S. Ill. U. L.J. 463 (2007)

A cornerstone principle of consumer bankruptcy law in the United States historically has been to provide "the honest but unfortunate debtor . . . a new opportunity in life and a clear field for future effort, unhampered by the pressure and discouragement of preexisting debt." [*Local Loan Co. v. Hunt*, 292 U.S. 234, 244 (1934).] Until 2005, this "fresh start" policy was implemented through the medium of a generous, immediate, and largely freely available chapter 7 discharge.

However, in 2005, the worm turned. In April 2005, Congress enacted and President Bush signed into law the Bankruptcy Abuse Prevention and Consumer Protection Act of 2005 ("BAPCPA"), effective for cases filed on or after October 17, 2005. In name and in substance, the 2005 Amendments to the Bankruptcy Code reveal an intent to restrict filings that are not made as a last resort. Illustrative of the rhetoric is a press release for the House Committee on the Judiciary, in which Rep. Rick Boucher contended that the then-existing Chapter 7 liquidation provisions allowed debtors to treat bankruptcy as just another "financial planning tool and file for bankruptcy for simple convenience."

The Bankruptcy Code currently in effect reflects an underlying concern that too many debtors who could afford to repay some of their debts were taking advantage of a forgiving bankruptcy regime to obtain a fresh start or "head start," to borrow the pejorative phrase of the day to the detriment of the economy, or at least of their creditors. The stated goal of the 2005 Amendments to the Bankruptcy Code was to restore integrity to the system by preventing "abuse." The main restorative vehicle was the "means test," which in § 707(b)(2) creates a presumption of "abuse" that dictates dismissal or conversion of a chapter 7 case for these "can-pay" consumer debtors. . . .

BAPCPA "replaces the presumption in favor of granting the relief sought by the debtor with a presumption that abuse exists" unless the debtor is able to prove, through extensive documentation, that he should be allowed a fresh start. The statutory "presumption of abuse", moreover, forces even honest but unfortunate debtors to rebut a moral charge against them.

NOTES AND QUESTIONS

1. The Purpose of the Biblical System of Debt Relief. The purpose of the American bankruptcy system historically, and at least in part, lined up with the purpose of the biblical system of debt relief as manifested in the Sabbath Year, i.e., a new beginning. Of this, Dr. R. J. Rushdoony writes:

> An important aspect of the year of release is that it means a year of renewed opportunity. God does not allow men, if they obey His law, to destroy their future indefinitely. In Joseph Parker's words,
>
>> We must have the element of hopefulness in life: without hope we die. Tomorrow will be a day of ransom and liberty—if not tomorrow by the clock, yet tomorrow in feeling: already the dawn is upon our hearts, already we hear noises of a distant approach: presently a great gladness will descend upon the soul. The child will be better in a day or two; when the weather warms (the doctor assures us), the life will be stronger. When arrangements now in progress are consummated—and they will be consummated presently—the whole house will be lighted up with real joy and thankfulness. So the spirit speaks to itself; so the heart sings songs in the night-time; so we live by hope and faith. . . .
>>
>> We find in this year of release what we all need—namely, the principle of new chances, new opportunities, fresh beginnings.

> Tomorrow—said the debtor or the slave—is the day of release, and the next day I shall begin again: I shall have another chance in life; the burden will be taken away, the darkness will be dispersed, and life shall be young again. Every man ought to have more chances than one, even in our own life. God has filled the sphere of life with opportunities. The expired week is dead and gone, and Christ's own resurrection day comes with the Gospel of hope, and the Gospel of a new beginning, the Gospel of a larger opportunity; and the year dies with proclamations from heaven, and Life says, when it is not utterly lost,—I will begin again: I will no longer blot the book of life: I will write with a steady and careful hand.

> Parker rightly stressed that the meaning of God's law here is to give His covenant people fresh opportunities.[8]

This quote both adequately and eloquently captures the hope, beauty, and invigorating grace of a new beginning and a fresh start.

This gracious legal provision also points us to and derives from an idea that is even more fundamental to all of creation—the gospel of the Lord Jesus Christ, which is portrayed as a release from slavery, a release from overwhelming debt, and freedom and rest in Christ. The biblical Sabbath Year and its concomitant release from debt and slavery pointed to that much greater release from debt and slavery to be found in Christ. *See, e.g., Luke* 4:18-19.

The Bible clearly teaches that all people are slaves to sin until and if they are set free from that slavery to be slaves to righteousness and to Christ. *See, e.g., Romans* 6. Just as the biblical debt relief system brought freedom from bondservice, the gospel brings freedom from bondservice or slavery to sin. "[6] We know that our old self was crucified with him in order that the body of sin might be brought to nothing, *so that we would no longer be enslaved to sin.* [7] For one who has died has been set free from sin." *Romans* 6:6-7 (English Standard Version) (emphasis added). "[17] But thanks be to God, that you *who were once slaves of sin* have become obedient from the heart to the standard of teaching to which you were committed [i.e., the gospel], [18] and, *having been set free from sin, have become slaves of righteousness. Id.* at 6:17-18 (emphasis added).

---

[8] ROUSAS JOHN RUSHDOONY, COMMENTARIES ON THE PENTATEUCH: DEUTERONOMY 225 (2008) (quoting JOSEPH PARKER, THE PEOPLE'S BIBLE, NUMBERS 27-DEUTERONOMY (Volume 4) 240–41 (n.d.)).

Therefore, every time a slave was set free (a manumission) under the Old Testament legal system, it taught something of the greater manumission from sin that would come through the death, burial, and resurrection of the Lord Jesus Christ.

Similarly, the Bible teaches that all people owe an overwhelming sin debt to God that could only be paid through the substitutionary atonement of Christ's death on the cross. *See, e.g., Matthew* 6:12, 18:21-35; *Colossians* 2:13-14. The Sabbath Year brought freedom from debts (even debts that resulted from grievous sin such as stealing), and the gospel brings freedom from the most grievous debt of all—the sin debt. "[3] And you, who were dead in your trespasses and the uncircumcision of your flesh, God made alive together with him, having forgiven us all our trespasses, [14] by canceling the record of debt that stood against us with its legal demands. This he set aside, nailing it to the cross." *Colossians* 2:13-14 (English Standard Version). The *ESV Study Bible* note on Colossians 2:14 is very helpful in amplifying Paul's point:

> In the Greco-Roman world, the "record of debt" (Gk. *cheirographon*) was a written note of indebtedness. Paul uses this as a word picture to characterize each person's indebtedness to God because of sin. God himself has mercifully resolved this problem for all who put their faith in Jesus by taking this note and **nailing it to the cross**, where Jesus paid the debt. The image comes from the notice fastened to a cross by the Roman authorities, declaring the crime for which the criminal was being executed (see John 19:19–22).[9]

Accordingly, every time a person's debts were forgiven under the Old Testament system of debt relief, it was a picture of the relief to be had in Christ from the awful sin debt owed to God.

Lastly, the Sabbath Year, and its related debt relief and manumission, was meant to grant freedom and rest to God's people. Both the Sabbath Day and the Sabbath Year taught this. In the New Testament, we are told that the Sabbath (presumably both the Sabbath Day and the Sabbath Year) find their ultimate fulfillment in the Lord Jesus Christ. Just as the freedom from debt and slavery should bring about a wonderful rest, so does the freedom from sin debt and slavery through the gospel bring about a wonderful rest. Again, the Old Testament law of Sabbath, or rest, taught about and pictured the coming rest in Christ.

In summary, the purpose of the biblical system of debt relief—giving the debtor freedom from debt and slavery and thereby a new

---

[9] THE ESV STUDY BIBLE 2297 (2008).

beginning—on a deeper level is actually to teach people about and point to salvation through the Lord Jesus Christ. Accordingly, the principle underlying the biblical system of debt relief is in a very real way the gospel.[10]

2. An Additional Purpose? The American bankruptcy system also carries an additional purpose; one that is not as frequently stated as the "fresh start" purpose. The additional purpose is the orderly distribution of the debtor's non-exempt assets to his creditors. This is meant to prevent the so-called race to the courthouse where all of the debtor's creditors race to the courthouse to file suit and obtain liens. Obviously, the lien priority system is based in large measure upon a winner-take-all, first-in-time-first-in-right type philosophy that results in those who get their liens first getting completely paid and those who are late comers in the race to the courthouse getting nothing. Thus, the bankruptcy system is thought to be more equitable in that it freezes the debtor's estate and equitably divides the assets among the various creditors. Accordingly, in the American system of debt relief, there is, in addition to the "fresh start" purpose, a repayment purpose. It is this repayment purpose that was at the heart of the BAPCPA's desire to prevent abuse.

3. Comparison of the Purpose of the Biblical System of Debt Relief with the American Bankruptcy System. As noted above, both the biblical system of debt relief and the American bankruptcy system share as an important purpose the granting of a second chance, a fresh start, to the debtor. However, the American system adds to this a repayment purpose that is not directly found in the biblical system.[11]

As the article excerpt at the beginning of this chapter points out, and as the Supreme Court has recently noted, the BAPCPA shifted the balance in the American bankruptcy system more toward repayment as opposed to a fresh start.

> "Congress enacted the . . . BAPCPA . . . to correct perceived abuses of the bankruptcy system." *Milavetz, Gallop & Milavetz, P.A. v. United States*, 559 U.S. 229, ——, 130 S.Ct. 1324, 1329, 176 L.Ed.2d 79 (2010). In particular,

---

[10] Which helps to explain why the biblical system of debt relief was only available to God's covenant people, the Israelites, and was not available to those outside of God's people. Those outside of Christ do not have freedom from slavery to sin and their sin debt has not been paid. Therefore, they do not enjoy freedom and rest in Christ.

[11] The Bible strongly encourages the repayment of debts. Therefore, this should not be seen as hostility toward the repayment of debts in general. Rather, the Sabbath Year debt relief system does not attempt to combine the goal of the repayment of just debts with the purpose of a fresh start as the American system does.

Congress adopted the means test—"[t]he heart of
[BAPCPA's] consumer bankruptcy reforms," H.R.Rep. No.
109–31, pt. 1, p. 2 (2005), and the home of the statutory
language at issue here—to help ensure that debtors who *can*
pay creditors *do* pay them. *See, e.g., ibid.* (under BAPCPA,
"debtors [will] repay creditors the maximum they can
afford").[12]

Since the goal of repayment is not even really present in the biblical debt
relief systems, a shift toward that goal in the American system requires
thoughtful Christian reflection and evaluation. Is such a shift a sign of a
movement away from biblical principles?

This question necessarily requires some determination regarding
abuse, the concern about which was at the heart of the BAPCPA reforms.
The fact that the American bankruptcy system is debtor-initiated, as
opposed to a set society-wide time of debt relief, arguably does open up the
potential for abuse in a way not present in the biblical system.

In the biblical system, everyone would be aware of the coming of
the Sabbath Year. "To protect both lender and borrower, the loan, one
assumes, was of such an amount as to reasonably be repaid in whatever
time remained until the year of cancellation [the Sabbath Year]. That is,
the size of the loan was commensurate with the time to repay it."[13] In fact,
given the nature of the system, God seems to have been more concerned
that lenders would be unwilling to lend as the Sabbath Year drew nigh as
opposed to debtors being able to abuse the system. *Deuteronomy* 15:7-11.

By contrast, in the American bankruptcy system, a creditor is never
quite sure when any particular debtor might file bankruptcy. Leaving the
timing of debt relief in the hands of debtors does open up the possibility of
opportunistic behavior or abuse of the system. Therefore, at least
arguably, the dual (and often competing goal) of repayment is warranted
in the American system. Further, and again arguably, a shift more
toward repayment was perhaps warranted in 2005.

A thorough consideration of this difference (debtor-initiated debt
relief v. society-wide at a particular time debt relief) and all of its
implications is beyond the scope of this chapter (and likely the ability of
this author.) Still, it seems that at least some consideration of this
important distinction between the two systems is critical in order to think
through this issue of purpose. However, this begs a deeper question:
maybe the discussion initially should be whether the American system
should switch to the biblical model of a set time of society-wide debt relief
as opposed to the current debtor-initiated system.

---

[12] *Ransom v. FIA Card Services, N.A.*, 559 U.S. ____, 131 S.Ct. 716, 721 (2011).
[13] Eugene H. Merrill, Deuteronomy, The New American Commentary
(Volume 4) 243 (1994).

Regardless, these are very important issues and questions. The law is undoubtedly didactic, meaning that it teaches people. It can either teach people good lessons about things that are God-honoring, righteous, and true, or it can teach people lies about the nature of the world and the God who made it. In this instance, it seems that debt relief is, in the Bible, very much tied up in teaching people about the gospel. Therefore, all Christians should be concerned about our system of debt relief and what it is teaching.

What do you think? What does our system of debt relief in America teach? Is it subject to abuse? What should be done about that abuse if so? Should we shift the purpose and focus more toward repayment, as the BAPCPA did, or should we look at fundamentally changing the system?

If we did shift to the biblical system of a set time of society-wide debt relief, what might that look like? Can you imagine it? Could it possibly work, or is our current system better?

_____

_____

_____

_____

_____

_____

CHAPTER 6
NONDISCHARGEABILITY AND THE BIBLICAL WORLDVIEW

In re Marlow
2013 WL 3515726 (E.D. Tenn. July 11, 2013)[1]

Robert Bentley Marlow has a law degree but no Tennessee law license. He also has nearly $250,000 in student loans that he asserts he cannot pay. After filing for bankruptcy, he sought a discharge of his student loans under 11 U.S.C. § 523(a)(8). The bankruptcy court found the debt was not dischargeable and granted summary judgment in favor of the United States Department of Education, Sallie Mae, Inc., the University of Tennessee, and Educational Credit Management Corporation (collectively, the "Appellees"). In making this ruling, the bankruptcy court found that Marlow could not satisfy the three prerequisites for relief under 11 U.S.C. § 523(a)(8). The bankruptcy court found Marlow had not maximized his income nor made a good faith effort to repay his student loans to the Appellees. Additionally, the bankruptcy found no additional circumstance indicating that Marlow's state of financial affairs is likely to persist for a significant portion of the repayment period.

Proceeding *pro se,* Marlow now appeals the decision of the bankruptcy court. Marlow argues that the bankruptcy court erred in its

---

[1] At the time this book went to print, the Westlaw citation was the only one available.

findings of fact and conclusions of law and that the Court should vacate the bankruptcy court's memorandum and judgment and remand for further proceedings. The Court has carefully reviewed the parties' briefs in light of the entire record and controlling law. For the reasons set forth below, the decision of the bankruptcy court will be affirmed and Marlow's appeal dismissed.

I.

Marlow was 31 years old at the time of the bankruptcy proceedings. By that time, he had several degrees. He earned a bachelor's degree in philosophy from the University of Tennessee in December 2001 and an associate's degree in paralegal studies from Roane State Community College in May 2004. He also earned a law degree from the Cumberland School of Law at Samford University in May 2009 and a master's degree in social and political philosophy from the University of Tennessee in May 2010. He financed these two advanced degrees with subsidized and unsubsidized federally funded student loans as well as private student loan obligations from the Appellees. The total of all loans to all Appellees at the time of the bankruptcy proceedings was $247,877.93.

After law school, Marlow failed the Tennessee bar exam in the summer of 2009. He took the exam again in February 2010, and he passed. The Tennessee Board of Law Examiners, however, did not admit him to the Tennessee bar. On April 2, 2010, Marlow was notified by letter that his application for bar admission had been place[d] [sic] under investigation for character and fitness concerns based on his prior citation for public intoxication and his sixteen motor vehicle citations. Then, on April 21, 2010, Marlow was arrested by the Knoxville City Police for public intoxication. The Board of Law Examiners issued a show cause order on May 18, 2010, directing Marlow to show why his application should not be denied on character and fitness grounds. Marlow responded, but upon the advice of his father and uncle, two Tennessee attorneys, he did not disclose his most recent arrest. By the time of Marlow's response, the Board of Law Examiners had received an anonymous tip about the recent arrest, and so it scheduled the first show cause hearing on the matter. Marlow appeared at this first hearing, and he explained that criminal charges from the April 20, 2010 arrest were ultimately dismissed. He rejected two monitoring agreements proposed by the Tennessee Lawyers Assistance Program, and he did not appear at a second show cause hearing because he was in Japan on a trip with his sister.

Ultimately, on June 27, 2011, the Board of Law Examiners determined Marlow should not be licensed to practice law in Tennessee. Marlow appealed the decision, and on February 12, 2012, the Tennessee Supreme Court affirmed the decision. Marlow has not sought admission to practice law in any other state, and he has no plans to do so. He has continued to appeal the licensing decision by filing a Petition for Writ of Certiorari with the United States Supreme Court, which was denied on October 1, 2012. Additionally, Marlow has pursued separate civil litigation against the Board of Law Examiners.

After receiving deferments in 2009 and 2010, Marlow made minimal payments to Sallie Mae, Inc. He did not make payments on the other loans. He sought forbearance from the University of Tennessee in November 2010 and February 2011, and he requested forbearance concerning the loans now held by Educational Credit Management Corporation. Since receiving his law and master's degrees, Marlow has not had steady employment. His primary financial support has come from his father. Since April 2007, Marlow has held the position of co-founder and managing member of Dogwood Creek Investments, LLC, a real estate development company in Knoxville, Tennessee. Marlow estimates that he has earned $125.00 per month from Dogwood Creek Investments since September 2010. This is the final position listed on Marlow's resume, which mostly reflects Marlow's time as a student, and thus the six other entries from 2002 to 2009 are part-time or temporary positions and externships. Since law school, Marlow also has been self-employed: he has worked landscaping, construction, and various odd jobs, sold beverages outside Neyland Stadium during University of Tennessee football games in the fall of 2009 and 2010, and collected scrap metal and aluminum cans. In 2011, he earned income from payments on [a] promissory note he issued on January 5, 2011. In 2012, like in 2011, his limited income included gifts from family and friends.

Marlow voluntarily filed for Chapter 7 bankruptcy protection on August 29, 2011, primarily for relief from his student loan debt, as well as some credit card debt. At that time, he listed in his bankruptcy schedules a total unsecured debt of $260,453.36, of he which listed $223,542.00 owed to the Appellees for student loans. Marlow then sought to discharge his student loan debt pursuant to 11 U.S.C. § 523(a)(8). The bankruptcy court determined that this debt could not be discharged, and this appeal followed.

* * *

III.

As Marlow correctly notes, the bankruptcy court's findings of fact are subject to a clearly erroneous standard of review, Bankruptcy Rule 8013, and its conclusions of law are subject to a *de novo* standard of review. *Oyler v. Educ. Credit Mgmt. Corp. (In re Oyler)*, 397 F.3d 382, 384 (6th Cir.2005). The Sixth Circuit Court of Appeals has stated that "[w]hether student loans pose an undue hardship is a legal question" for *de novo* review. *Id.*

Student loan debt may be discharged only when repayment "will impose an undue hardship on the debtor and the debtor's dependents." 11 U.S.C. § 523(a)(8). The Sixth Circuit has adopted the *Brunner* test for undue hardship which requires a three-part showing:

> (1) that the debtor cannot maintain, based on current income and expenses, a 'minimal' standard of living for herself and her dependents if forced to repay the loans;

> (2) that additional circumstances exist indicating that this state of affairs is likely to persist for a significant portion of the repayment period of the student loans; and

> (3) that the debtor has made good faith efforts to repay the loans.

Tirch v. Pa. Higher Educ. Assistance Auth. (In re Tirch), 409 F.3d 677, 680 (6th Cir.2005) (quoting *Brunner v. N.Y. State Higher Educ. Serv. Corp.*, 831 F.2d 395 (2d Cir.1987)); *Oyler*, 397 F.3d at 385. "If a plaintiff cannot satisfy even one of these criteria, then she is not entitled to a finding of undue hardship." *Miller v. Pa. Higher Educ. Assistance Agency (In re Miller)*, No. 3:05–cv–38, 2005 WL 2127931, at *3 (E.D.Tenn. Aug.31, 2005). Upon review of the record, the Court finds that the bankruptcy court correctly concluded that Marlow cannot meet his burden under all of the prongs of the *Brunner* test.

To satisfy the first prong, a debtor must show that he strives to minimize his expenses and maximize his income. After reviewing the undisputed facts taken from Marlow's own discovery responses, and citing Marlow's own admissions, the bankruptcy court found that Marlow had minimized his expenses but failed to maximize his income. The bankruptcy emphasized that he admitted to performing only a "cursory look for jobs on several online jobs boards and found no jobs that match his credentials" since February 2012. This "cursory look" was the result of his choice to devote his time to *pro se* lawsuits against the Tennessee Supreme Court and its members, the Tennessee Board of Law Examiners and its members, the Tennessee Attorney General, the City of Knoxville, and the officer who arrested him. In addition, the bankruptcy court noted that Marlow had not sought to obtain a law license outside Tennessee nor had he sought employment outside of Knoxville, where he resides. Overall, the bankruptcy court found Marlow's pursuit of employment to be limited at best, and this Court agrees. Marlow's own discovery responses and admissions create a clear record showing a failure to maximize his income, and so he has failed to satisfy the first of the *Brunner* prongs.

The second prong of the *Brunner* test requires a debtor to show that additional circumstances exist indicating that the state of affairs that prevents him from repaying his student loans is likely to persist for a significant portion of the repayment period. The focus, therefore, is on "permanency or, what can be termed, an involuntary inability to improve one's financial circumstances." *Storey v. Nat'l Enter. Sys. (In re Storey),* 312 B.R. 867, 871 (Bankr.N.D.Ohio 2004). To meet this prong, Marlow must show "a certainty of hopelessness, not merely a present inability to fulfill financial commitment." *Tirch,* 409 F.3d at 681; *Oyler,* 397 F.3d at 386. The Sixth Circuit has explained that the additional circumstances "may include illness, disability, a lack of useable job skills, or the existence of a large number of dependents." *Oyler,* 397 F.3d at 386. Above all, the additional circumstances "must be beyond the debtor's control, not borne of free choice." *Id.; see also Barrett v. Educ. Credit Mgmt. Corp. (In re Barrett),* 487 F.3d 353, 358 (6th Cir.2007).

In this case, Marlow is not suffering from any illness or disability, and he has no dependents. At the time of the bankruptcy proceedings, he was 31 years old. He is clearly well-educated. He has useable job skills, including his training as a paralegal. Here, Marlow offers the denial of his application for a Tennessee law license as an additional circumstance indicating his financial situation is likely to persist. The bankruptcy court held that this was not the type of circumstance required under *Brunner,* and this Court agrees. The denial of his application was the result of actions taken by Marlow, actions "borne of free choice." Marlow has not provided evidence that his lack of a law license makes him unemployable in any of his fields of expertise. "The Court, therefore, cannot say that [his] past will inevitably and ultimately result in a complete restriction, as opposed to a potential narrowing, of job opportunities in [his] profession." *Nixon v. Key Educ. Res. (In re Nixon),* 453 B.R. 311, 332 (Bankr.S.D.Ohio 2011) (discussing a debtor whose degree was revoked for plagiarism). Moreover, the record is clear that Marlow has not sufficiently sought to maximize his income. The bankruptcy court examined this record in detail and concluded that Marlow has not presented evidence that he exhausted all reasonable efforts to obtain non-legal employment. Marlow's efforts actually were focused on his *pro se* litigation, not finding employment. Given the clearly supported facts, the existence of Marlow's financial circumstances do not evidence an undue hardship.

The third prong of the *Brunner* test requires a debtor to show that he has made good faith efforts to repay his student loans. In finding that Marlow had not attempted to repay his loans in good faith, the bankruptcy court considered factors drawn from *Hart v. Educ. Credit Mgmt. Corp. (In re Hart),* 438 B.R. 406, 413 (E.D.Mich.2010):

(1) whether the failure to repay the student loan was due to circumstances beyond the debtor's reasonable control; (2) whether the debtor has used all available resources to repay the loan; (3) whether the debtor is using her best efforts to maximize her earnings potential; (4) how long after the loan was incurred did the debtor seek to discharge the debts; (5) what the overall percentage of the student loan debt is compared to debtor's overall debt; and (6) whether or not the debtor has gained tangible benefits of the student loan.

Here, the factors clearly support the bankruptcy court's determination. As discussed above, Marlow's failure to repay is not beyond his reasonable control. He has declined to apply for an income contingent repayment plan, so he has not used all available resources to repay the loans. Marlow has made almost no payments on his loans, turning to the bankruptcy court for relief just over a year after obtaining his fourth degree. Marlow's student loan debt comprises the majority (approximately 86%) of his overall debt, and he has received a tangible benefit from these student loans in the form of two advanced degrees.

Considering the record, especially the timing of his bankruptcy filing, his minimal payments, and his failure to seek income-based repayment plans, Marlow has failed to show he made a good faith effort to repay his loans. *See also Fields v. Sallie Mae Serv. Corp., et al. (In re Fields)*, 286 F. App'x 246, 251 ("Moreover, because Fields declined even to apply for [income contingent repayment] relief, she has failed to sustain the 'heavy burden' under *Tirch* of proving that she made a good faith effort to repay her loans."). The Court therefore agrees with the bankruptcy court that Marlow cannot meet the third prong of the *Brunner* test.

As discussed above, a debtor must meet all three *Brunner* prongs to be eligible for an undue hardship discharge of his student loans. This Court agrees with the bankruptcy court that there is no genuine dispute of material fact that would enable Marlow to meet his burden with respect to every *Brunner* prong, and thus summary judgment in favor of the Appellees was proper. Accordingly, the Court affirms the opinion of the bankruptcy court, and Appellant Robert Bentley Marlow's appeal will be dismissed.

NOTES AND QUESTIONS

1. What Do You Think? Do you agree with the Court, or would you have ruled differently? Does Mr. Marlow deserve a discharge of his student loans, or should he be forced to pay them? Why? If he does deserve a discharge, should it be partial or complete?

_____

_____

_____

_____

_____

2. A Growing Problem? Student loan debt has likely reached a crisis level on America. It is widely recognized by a number of sources, including the Federal Reserve Bank of New York and the Consumer Finance Protection Bureau, that student loan debt exceeds $900 billion and may well be at or over $1 trillion. That exceeds credit card debt, auto loan debt, and home equity line of credit debt. Only home mortgage debt exceeds student loan debt for American households.[2]

Further, it is estimated that in excess of 25% of student loans have past due balances. Accordingly, it seems likely that there will be many, many more borrowers with student loan debt hoping to discharge all or part of their balances in bankruptcy. Many of these borrowers were undoubtedly strongly encouraged to pursue post-secondary or even post-graduate education, and, indeed, it is government policy that they should be so encouraged. That being said, does it make sense to except student loans from discharge? What policy is behind § 523(a)(8)? Do you agree with it? To put it another way, why are student loans treated differently than credit cards, auto loans, or home loans?

_____

_____

_____

_____

_____

3. What Should the Test for Undue Hardship Be? "There has been a wide range of judicial reaction to the undue hardship claims of debtors. [However, t]he most widely used test for evaluating the

---

[2] A simple Google search will reveal a number of sources on this topic, including the estimated number of student loans that are in arrears.

dischargeability of a student loan under section 523(a)(8)" is the *Brunner* test, which has been adopted by the Sixth Circuit and was applied by the Court in the preceding case. 4 *Collier on Bankruptcy* ¶ 523.14[2] (Alan N. Resnick & Henry J. Sommer eds., 16th ed. 2009).

Commenting on § 523(a)(8) and the federal courts' handling thereof, *Collier on Bankruptcy*[3] states

> Despite the courts' best efforts to formulate objective criteria for evaluating undue hardship, the application of the articulated standards necessarily requires each court to apply its own intuitive sense of what is a "minimal" standard of living and what is "good faith." At bottom, *the Bankruptcy Code requires bankruptcy courts to decide how much personal sacrifice society expects from individuals who accepted the benefits of guaranteed student loans but who have not obtained the financial rewards they had hoped to receive as a result of their educational expenditures.*

Id. (emphasis added.)

Under § 523(a)(8) and Sixth Circuit precedent, there is no question that the Court arrived at the right answer in the preceding case. It correctly applied the *Brunner* test as adopted by the Sixth Circuit. That said, do you agree with the law on this point? Should it be more forgiving or less? Or, is it about right? Is this an objective standard that can be applied justly across all cases, or it is too subjective? To paraphrase the words of *Collier on Bankruptcy*, how much personal sacrifice should be expected of individuals who have accepted the benefits of guaranteed students loans and found themselves unable to repay?

_____

_____

_____

_____

_____

   4. Factors v. Elements. Some tests articulated by courts contain factors and others contain elements. The distinction is important. A test based upon factors typically requires a weighing of the various factors, but not all factors must be found in order for the test to have been met and typically no one factor is determinative. By contrast, in a test based upon elements, all elements must be satisfied.

---

[3] *Collier on Bankruptcy* is probably the leading treatise on bankruptcy law.

The case above contains an example of both types of tests. Which test is based upon elements? Which one is based upon factors? Can you tell how this makes a difference? *See, e.g., In re Fields*, 286 Fedd.Appx. 246, 251 (6th Cir. 2007) (*citing In re Oyler*, 397 F.3d 382, 386-386 (6th Cir. 2005)).

---

5. Discharge in the Biblical Debt Relief System. In the biblical system of debt relief, discharge appears to be complete. In other words, determinations of dischargeability are not made in the biblical debt relief systems because all debts appear to be subject to discharge. As noted in previous chapters, the biblical system forgives all debts however incurred. This is very much like the gospel, which forgives all of the sin debt owed regardless of the type of sins that comprise that debt. *See, e.g., Mark* 3:28-29 ("[a]ll sins shall be forgiven unto the sons of men, and blasphemies wherewith soever they shall blaspheme"); 1 *John* 1:9 ("[i]f we confess our sins, he is faithful and just to forgive us *our* sins, and to cleanse us from all unrighteousness"); and 1 *Corinthians* 6:11 (after listing off a number of heinous sins, Paul tells the Corinthians "such were some of you: but ye are washed, but ye are sanctified, but ye are justified in the name of the Lord Jesus, and by the Spirit of our God").[4]

Accordingly, it could be argued that a just system of debt relief based upon the biblical model would also forgive all debts. Discharge would therefore be complete, and there would be no issues of nondischargeability. However, as noted in the previous chapter, this raises the very challenging issue of the primary difference between the biblical system of debt relief and the American bankruptcy system, i.e., the fact that the American system is debtor-initiated as opposed to being society wide as in the biblical system. How should this difference impact the American bankruptcy system? Is a concern with nondischargeability legitimate given the fact that bankruptcy is debtor-initiated and therefore more subject to abuse by debtors? Or, regardless of this difference, should the American system still provide for a complete discharge?

Beyond this difference, another difference should be considered in making this determination. The biblical system also provides for more

---

[4] The unforgivable sin described in *Mark* 3:29, in the opinion of the author, is the one exception, which can only be committed by one so hardened that salvation through Christ has already been undeniably rejected.

robust (to say the least) debt collection methods. Under the biblical system, one could be sold into bondservice if he could not pay for his debts. *See, e.g., Deuteronomy* 15:12-18, *Leviticus* 25:35-55, and 2 *Kings* 4:1-7. His service (or the price of his service) would help to repay what he owed.

Obviously, in the present case, Mr. Marlow (or his father) would be much more interested in paying his debts if he thought he would be sold into bondservice if he could not pay. Further, he would likely have been much more cautious with regard to both incurring the debt and engaging in activities that cost him the opportunity to become a licensed attorney and to practice law.

Since debt collection methods under the biblical system were more drastic, a broader discharge was perhaps justified. On the other hand, in our system, where debt collection methods are not so robust, more of a focus on debt repayment, in addition to a fresh start for the debtor, coupled with the nondischargeability of certain debts is perhaps necessary. What do you think? Does this difference in debt collection possibilities between the biblical and American systems necessitate differences with regard to both the purpose of bankruptcy and the issue of the scope of the discharge available? Which system is more just? Which system do you prefer?

_____

_____

_____

_____

_____

_____

CHAPTER 7
TITHING IN CHAPTER 13 PLANS

The idea that gifts can be avoided by creditors, or, to put it another way, creditors must be paid before gifts can be made, has ancient roots in Anlgo-American law. *See, e.g.,* Statute of 13 Elizabeth, Chapter 5 (1570). As the Kentucky high court once said, "[a] debtor must be just before he is generous." *Creel v. Cloyd*, 152 S.W. 776, 777 (Ky. 1913.)

Despite these ancient origins, it is not clear that this policy was often or always applied to gifts to churches. Historically, there would have been a healthy degree of stigma against suing churches that would have likely kept many creditors and bankruptcy trustees from attempting to recover a contribution made to a church, often referred to as tithes and offerings, alms, or merely tithes. However, perhaps surprisingly, this specific issue—tithes paid to churches by debtors in or near bankruptcy—generated very little interest (or case law) until relatively recently. The following case deals with this issue in the context of the confirmation of a Chapter 13 plan.

In re Krischner
259 B.R. 416 (Bankr. M.D. Fl. 2001)

FINDINGS OF FACT

On March 9, 2000, Debtors filed for Chapter 13 bankruptcy protection.

[In an omitted portion of the opinion, the Court recounts various filings in the case and notes that the Debtors plan includes an amount of approximately nine percent of their gross income for charitable contributions to their church.]

. . . Trustee argues that some of the charitable contribution expense was not reasonably necessary for Debtors' maintenance and support and therefore constituted unapplied disposable income under 11 U.S.C. § 1325(b). Trustee further asserts that the excessive charitable contribution evidenced Debtors' lack of good faith in proposing a Chapter 13 plan to deal with their creditors pursuant to 11 U.S.C. § 1325(a)(3).

Neither side presented any evidence as to the sincerity of the religious beliefs motivating Debtors' charitable contributions. Neither party brought forward any evidence as to Debtors' history of charitable giving.

CONCLUSIONS OF LAW

The Court divides the issues before it into two questions presented. First, may a Debtors' charitable contributions be treated as disposable income that must be distributed to creditors under § 1325(b)? Second, may evidence of a reservation of a charitable contribution expense alone establish a lack of good faith sufficient to deny confirmation pursuant to § 1325(a)(3)?

I. CHARITABLE CONTRIBUTIONS AS DISPOSABLE INCOME

A. The disposable income standard and charitable donation "exemption"

Under 11 U.S.C. § 1325(b), a debtor must contribute all of his disposable income into a Chapter 13 plan if a trustee or unsecured creditor objects to confirmation of the plan. Section 1325(b) provides, in relevant part:

> (b)(1) If the trustee or the holder of an allowed unsecured claim objects to the confirmation of the plan, then the court may not approve the plan unless, as of the effective date of the plan—
>> (A) the value of the property to be distributed under the plan on account of such claim is not less than the amount of such claim; or
>> (B) the plan provides that all of the debtor's projected disposable income to be received in the three-year period beginning on the date that the first payment is due under the plan will be applied to make payments under the plan.
> (2) For purposes of this subsection, "disposable income" means income which is received by the debtor and which is not reasonably necessary to be expended—

(A) for the maintenance or support of the debtor or a dependent of the debtor, including charitable contributions (that meet the definition of "charitable contribution" under section 548(d)(3)) to a qualified religious or charitable entity or organization (as that term is defined in section 548(d)(4)) in an amount not to exceed 15 percent of the gross income of the debtor for the year in which the contributions are made . . .

11 U.S.C. § 1325(b)(2001). Section 548(d) provides, in relevant part:

(d)(3) In this section, the term "charitable contribution" means a charitable contribution, as that term is defined in section 170(c) of the Internal Revenue Code of 1986, if that contribution—
(A) is made by a natural person; and
(B) consists of—
(i) a financial instrument . . .; or
(ii) cash.
(d)(4) In this section, the term "qualified religious or charitable entity or organization" means—
(A) an entity described in section 170(c)(1) of the Internal Revenue Code of 1986; or
(B) an entity or organization described in section 170(c)(2) of the Internal Revenue Code of 1986.

11 U.S.C. § 548(d) (2001).

Congress added the provision for charitable contributions to the definition of "disposable income" in the Religious Liberty and Charitable Donation Act of 1998 ("the RLCDA"), Pub.L. No. 105–183. The RLCDA attempted to overrule those bankruptcy courts that found that charitable contributions were per se not reasonably necessary for the support or maintenance of a debtor and thus constituted § 1325(b)(1) disposable income that must be applied to Chapter 13 plan payments. *See Drummond v. Cavanagh (In re Cavanagh)*, 250 B.R. 107, 111 (9th Cir. BAP 2000). Congress intended for the RLCDA to "protect the rights of debtors to continue to make religious and charitable contributions after they file for bankruptcy relief."

The Court finds it useful to characterize the RLDCA charitable contribution provision as a sort of "exemption." The RLDCA essentially provided that qualified charitable contributions, in an amount less than a certain percentage of a debtor's income, may not be "attached" by a trustee or an unsecured creditor seeking more distribution under a Chapter 13 plan, in the same way that a debtor may not be obligated to contribute to a Chapter 13 plan funds conclusively exempted under 11 U.S.C. § 522(1).

B. The split over a vestigial "reasonably necessary" requirement

Unfortunately Congress did not place the RLDCA charitable contribution "exemption" in a stand-alone subsection. The "exemption" was placed in subsection (b)(2)(A), which remains qualified by the phrase "reasonably necessary to be expended." Some courts write this off as a drafting oversight and find that a qualified contribution of less than fifteen percent of a debtor's gross income need not undergo "reasonably necessary" scrutiny. *See Cavanagh*, 250 B.R. at 112. Once qualified under § 548(d), a proposed charitable contribution expense becomes per se reasonably necessary and "exempt" from the "disposable income" objections of creditors and trustees. *See id.* "The clear and unmistakable message [of the RLDCA] is that the interests of creditors are subordinate to the interests of charitable organizations, and we must follow this mandate." *Id.* at 113.

Other courts, however, find that, in addition to the § 548(d) qualifications and fifteen percent limit, a charitable contribution must also be itself "reasonably necessary" in order to be "exempted" from treatment as disposable income. *See In re Buxton*, 228 B.R. 606, 610 (Bankr.W.D.La.1999). "The definition of 'disposable income' still contains the 'reasonably necessary' restriction . . . such [necessary] living expenses may *include* charitable contributions . . . [t]hose expenses, however, must still be determined by the court to be reasonable." *Id.* at 610 (italics original). The *Buxton* court reasoned that Congress did not intend to establish an automatic 15% "exemption," but rather intended to prevent courts from finding charitable contributions per se unreasonable. *See id.*

C. Rejection of the vestigial "reasonably necessary" requirement

The Court finds the reasoning of the *Cavanagh* decision more persuasive, and therefore concludes that a § 548(d)-qualified charitable contribution, whether "reasonably necessary" or not, may not be treated as unapplied disposable income if the contribution amounts to less than fifteen percent of a debtor's gross income.

The main difficulty with the vestigial reasonability requirement adopted in *Buxton* is that it completely obviates the intended goal of the RLDCA, namely to protect certain charitable contributions from the consideration-based, cost/benefit oriented disposable income test. Congress, in enacting the RLDCA, recognized that, compared to the sort of expenses generally considered reasonably necessary, such as electricity, food and transportation, charitable contributions would always look unreasonable, because a debtor receives no legal consideration for them.

Congress enacted the RLDCA in order to create a "safe haven," an "exemption," to protect a debtor's ability to make some charitable donations after filing for bankruptcy despite the lack of consideration received in exchange for those outlays. Allowing a court to apply a "reasonably necessary" qualification to the charitable contributions provision would thwart that stated purpose of the RLDCA. Courts would be compelled by precedent and common sense to conclude that a religious gift could never be reasonably necessary for support in the same economic sense as food expenditures or the cost of transport to a place of employment. The only lasting effect of the RLDCA would be to deprive courts of the power to find all such contributions unnecessary as a matter of law and thus provide a debtor with a futile evidentiary hearing at which to defend his contributions as reasonably necessary. Surely Congress did not intend the RLDCA to serve such a limited purpose.

The Court in *Buxton* feared that a charitable contribution "exemption" freed from the reasonableness requirement would create an opportunity for limitless abuse by debtors seeking to hide discretionary income from creditors. "Congress . . . must have intended some limitation on a debtor's right to make charitable contributions . . ." *Buxton*, 228 B.R. at 610.

There is no need to preserve the "reasonably necessary" requirement on such grounds, however, because more rational limitations do exist. The first limitation is obvious: Congress explicitly limited the religious giving "exemption" to fifteen percent of a debtor's gross income. The Court also thinks it appropriate to limit potential abuse by providing for monitoring of contributions in order to insure that the stated charitable donations are actually made to a qualified religious entity rather than used as discretionary spending by a debtor. Finally, any attempt by a debtor to claim an amount as "exempt" from treatment as disposable income under the RLDCA must pass the good faith test found in § 1325(a)(3).

Therefore the Court adopts a three-step test for "exemption" of charitable contributions from treatment as disposable income under § 1325(b)(2)(A). First, a contribution must be a "charitable contribution" as defined by § 548(d)(3). Second, a contribution must be made to a "qualified religious or charitable entity or organization" as defined by § 548(d)(4). Finally, a court may not confirm a proposed Chapter 13 plan that provides for a § 548(d)-qualified contribution in excess of fifteen percent of a debtor's gross income.[1]

---

[1] The Court here notes the distinction between its conclusions here and its findings in *In re Burgos*, 248 B.R. 446 (Bankr.M.D.Fla.2000). In *Burgos*, the court found

D. Application to the instant case

1. Qualification as a "charitable contribution" and as a "religious or charitable entity" under § 548(d)

Neither party brought forward evidence or addressed these standards at the hearing or in their submissions. Trustee did not assert that the charitable contributions proposed in Debtors' Schedule I were not IRS-qualified or that the church Debtor intended to give to was not IRS-qualified. Therefore the Court finds that Debtors' proposed contribution satisfies the § 548(d) standards. Debtors' failure to apply that portion of their income dedicated to charitable contributions may not justify denial of confirmation on unapplied disposable income grounds unless the amount to be contributed exceeds fifteen percent of Debtors' gross income.

2. The fifteen percent limitation

Debtors' proposed contributions do not exceed fifteen percent of Debtors' gross income. Debtors assert a contribution expense of $674.00 per month, according to their second Amended Schedule J. Debtors' gross monthly income is $ 7,147.19, according to their Amended Schedule I. Debtors propose to spend just over nine percent of their gross income on charitable contributions, well under the fifteen percent cap.[2] Therefore, Debtors' planned charitable contribution expenditure falls within the amount allowed by § 1325(b)(2)(A), and that amount will not be considered unapplied disposable income.

The Court will now proceed to the merits of Trustee's second objection, namely that Debtors' intent to reserve a charitable contribution expense evidences a lack of good faith in light of the amount of unsecured debt Debtors intend to discharge.

---

the expense of sending debtor's children to a private religious school "reasonably necessary" under § 1325(b). *See id.* at 450. In the instant case, the Court concludes that religious contributions qualified under § 548(d) need not undergo the "reasonably necessary" determination at all, because Congress intended to elevate such contributions above the "reasonably necessary" test. Congress has yet to so protect tuition expenses for religious private schools. The fact that such schools provide consideration—an education—in exchange for such reserved expense indicates that such tuition expenses may be "reasonably necessary" in their own right (as the Court concluded in *Burgos*) without a congressional "exemption."

[2] The Court notes that Debtors have risked violating a somewhat higher mandate by trimming their religious contribution below ten percent of their gross income in order to get their Chapter 13 Plan confirmed. "To whom also Abraham gave a tenth part of all; first being by interpretation king of righteousness, and after that also King of Salem, which is, King of peace." *Hebrews* 7:2.

II. CHARITABLE CONTRIBUTIONS AS EVIDENCE OF A LACK OF GOOD FAITH

In order to qualify for confirmation, a Chapter 13 Plan must satisfy all of the requirements of § 1325. The Court's finding that Debtors' charitable contributions do not violate the § 1325(b) disposable income test does not preclude successful opposition to Debtors' plan on other grounds. Nor does the invocation of a Congressional "exemption" prevent the use of the proposed "exempt" expenditure as evidence of a lack of good faith under § 1325(a)(3).

A. The § 1325(a)(3) good faith standard

1. Relevance of reservation of property or income "exempt" from treatment as disposable income

The reservation of a qualified charitable contribution expense, although an allocation protected from the disposable income inquiry under § 1325(b), may nevertheless evidence a lack of good faith in proposing a Chapter 13 plan under § 1325(a)(3). *See Cavanagh*, 250 B.R. at 114. As the *Cavanagh* court stated,

> Although the plain language of § 1325(b)(2)(A) does not restrict the timing of a debtor's tithing or prevent a debtor from increasing the amount of a charitable contribution on the eve of bankruptcy or after a bankruptcy petition is filed, these are factors that ought to be taken into consideration when looking at the totality of the circumstances to determine whether a debtor has proposed a chapter 13 plan in good faith and in compliance with § 1325(a)(3).

Id. As the Court previously noted in reviewing another sort of per se "indisposable" income, "although the personal injury settlement became conclusively exempt, and perhaps conclusively 'indisposable' . . . the Court maintained the power to withhold confirmation of the Plan on § 1325(a)(3) good faith grounds until the moment of confirmation."

2. Sincerity of belief as a factor in cases where a reserved charitable contribution expense is advanced as evidence of a lack of good faith

First, the Court finds relevant to the good faith inquiry the sincerity of a debtor's intent to actually make the proposed charitable contributions. The *Cavanagh* court, in finding that a debtor proposed in good faith a plan reserving a qualified charitable contribution expense, found that the bankruptcy court observed the debtor's demeanor sufficiently to support its finding that the debtor's religious beliefs were sincere and that the debtor had not "suddenly found God" as claimed by the objecting trustee. *See Cavanagh*, 250 B.R. at 113. The *Cavanagh* court found that this "sincerity test" effectively thwarts attempts by unscrupulous debtors to hide extra discretionary income under the guise of the charitable contribution "exemption." *See id.*

3. The *Kitchens* "totality of the circumstances" test

The Court also finds it necessary to analyze a proposed charitable contribution expense in the context of the "totality of the circumstances" good faith standard adopted by the Eleventh Circuit in *Kitchens v. Georgia R.R. Bank and Trust Co. (In re Kitchens)*, 702 F.2d 885 (11th Cir.1983). The *Buxton* court focused on similar all-purpose good faith factors in finding that a debtor should be denied confirmation based upon the size of the proposed charitable contributions in relation to the extent of debtor's unsecured debts and the amount of proposed plan payments. *See Buxton*, 228 B.R. at 611.

The *Kitchens* court set down eleven factors to be considered in determining whether, under the totality of the circumstances, a debtor proposed a Chapter 13 plan in good faith:

(1) the amount of the debtor's income from all sources;
(2) the living expenses of the debtor and his dependents;
(3) the amount of attorneys' fees;
(4) the probable or expected duration of the debtor's chapter 13 plan;
(5) the motivations of the debtor and his sincerity in seeking relief under the provisions of chapter 13;
(6) the debtor's degree of effort;
(7) the debtor's ability to earn and the likelihood of fluctuation in his earnings;
(8) special circumstances such as inordinate medical expense;
(9) the frequency with which the debtor has sought relief under the Bankruptcy Reform Act and its predecessors;
(10) the circumstances under which the debtor has contracted his debts and his demonstrated bona fides, or lack of same, in dealings with his creditors;
(11) the burden which the plan's administration would place on the trustee.

Kitchens, 702 F.2d at 888–89.

B. Application to the instant case

1. The "sincerity" inquiry

The Court finds that Debtors sincerely intend to make the charitable contributions listed in their amended Schedule J. Debtors indicated their intent to reserve some of their income for charitable contributions on their original Schedule I. Absent any evidence to the contrary, this indication satisfies the Court that Debtors gave to their church prepetition and merely intend to continue giving to their church postpetition. There is no evidence before the Court tending to show that Debtors invented the charitable contribution expense solely to keep extra discretionary income outside their creditors' grasp.

2. The *Kitchens* "totality of the circumstances" test

The Court finds that the totality of the circumstances indicate that Debtors proposed the Third Amended Plan in good faith. Trustee failed to bring forward sufficient evidence to convince the Court that confirmation of Debtors' Third Amended Plan would constitute an abuse of the provisions of Chapter 13. Debtors' Third Amended Plan provides for a relatively large twenty-one percent distribution to unsecured creditors. Debtors' adjusted expenses appear reasonable on their face, and Trustee failed to bring specific evidence on the excessiveness of any of them. Debtors do not appear to be keeping any extravagant assets. Debtors do not propose to discharge any debts nondischargeable under Chapter 7.

The relative size of the qualified charitable contribution expense alone cannot justify a finding of lack of good faith, much as the reservation of a valuable piece of exempt property or lucrative exempt income stream alone cannot justify such a finding. Trustee presented no evidence of a lack of good faith besides Debtors' intent to make charitable contributions, the amount of unsecured debt to be discharged, and the length of the Third Amended Plan. Trustee failed to bring forward any evidence tending to show that Debtors did not sincerely desire to pay off as much as reasonably possible to their unsecured creditors during the span of a standard three-year Chapter 13 plan. Trustee simply made bare assertions that Debtors could afford to pay more and suggested that an additional amount should come out of the "exempt" charitable contribution expense. Such an assertion without more constitutes mere second-guessing and does not justify denial of confirmation.

Therefore, the Court finds that Debtors proposed the Third Amended Plan in good faith and that the Plan should be confirmed.

III.   MONITORING   OF   DEBTORS'   CHARITABLE CONTRIBUTIONS

The Court finds that, although Debtors' charitable contributions do not constitute unapplied disposable income and do not indicate lack of good faith so as to prevent confirmation, Debtors should be obliged to provide documentation to Trustee that the amount allocated to charitable expenses is actually given to the § 548(d)-qualified charitable entity. Such proof should be easy to provide. For example, Debtors could request that their church provide them with a receipt for their contributions, as it provides a receipt for those seeking tax deductions for charitable giving. Debtors will supply Trustee with documentation of their contributions along with their monthly plan payments. Trustee may file any motion she deems appropriate to enforce these monitoring provisions.

CONCLUSION

The Court finds that Debtors' § 548(d)-qualified charitable contribution expenses of less than fifteen percent of their gross income may not be treated as unapplied disposable income in order to justify denial of confirmation on § 1325(b) grounds. The Court also finds that the size of Debtors' proposed charitable contributions alone does not sufficiently evidence a lack of good faith in order to justify denial of confirmation on § 1325(a)(3) grounds. The Court finally concludes that it is appropriate to mandate that Debtors provide documentation of their charitable giving to Trustee in order to ensure that Debtors are not fraudulently using the income allocated for charitable contributions as discretionary funds.

Trustee will prepare and submit an Order Confirming Plan in accordance with these Findings of Fact and Conclusions of Law, including a provision requiring Debtors to submit such proof as will satisfy Trustee that Debtors are actually making the proposed charitable contributions to a § 548(d)-qualified entity.

NOTES AND QUESTIONS

1. What Do You Think? What do you think? Do you think that debtors in cases such as the above should be able to "exempt" their tithes from disposable income that must be paid to the trustee and ultimately to creditors? Or, should "[a] debtor must be [required to be] just before he is generous." *Creel v. Cloyd*, 152 S.W. 776, 777 (Ky. 1913)?

Those questions deal with the existence of the "exemption" for charitable contributions, i.e., prudentially speaking, should Congress have passed such a measure. Beyond that, assuming the Bankruptcy Code as it currently exists, do you agree with the Courts in *Krischner* and *Cavanagh* or *Buxton*? Should a debtor have to prove that his or her tithes are reasonably necessary? Can that even be done? If so, how?

_____

_____

_____

_____

_____

2. Is Tithing Required? The Erdman's Bible Dictionary defines "tithe" as "[t]he dedication of a tenth of agricultural products, of livestock, of goods gained in trade, or of booty to the worship of a deity or to the persons who served that worship. This was a common custom in the ancient world."[3] The Old Testament deals extensively with the issue of tithes and the presenting of offerings. *See, e.g., Genesis* 14:20, 28:22; *Leviticus* 27:30-33; *Numbers* 18:21-32; *Deuteronomy* 26:12-14; *Nehemiah* 10:37-38, and *Malachi* 3:8-10. Generally speaking, it is one-tenth of one's increase.

The New Testament also mentions tithing. *See, e.g., Matthew* 23:23; *Luke* 11:42; and, as the Court notes in a footnote above, *Hebrews* 7:2. However, there is some dispute among Christians as to whether the tithe is still required of New Testament believers. Of this, R. J. Rushdoony writes:

> A common objection to tithing is that the New Testament supposedly sets a new and voluntary standard, whereby men give as they are able. The supposed authority for this is 2 *Corinthians* 8:12, and 9:7. But the statement in its original form is in *Deuteronomy* 16:17: "Every man shall give as he is able, according to the blessing of the Lord thy God which he hath given unto thee." The law here does not negate tithing: it has reference to the due proportion of our prosperity as something which is due to the Lord who gives it. Tithes *and* gifts are basic to both Testaments.[4]

---

[3] THE EERDMANS BIBLE DICTIONARY 1008 (1987).

[4] Rousas John Rushdoony, THE INSTITUTES OF BIBLICAL LAW, VOLUME TWO: LAW AND SOCIETY 700 (2001).

What do you think? Are Christians required to tithe or are Christians just required to give as they are able? If it is just as they are able, how much is a person filing bankruptcy able to give? How might this matter in cases such as the one above?

_____

_____

_____

_____

_____

3. Tithing in Good Faith? The Court concluded that charitable contributions still must be made (and planned) in good faith. Therefore, tithes must be made and planned in good faith, which, according to the Court, means that they must be made pursuant to a sincerely held religious belief. What proof should be taken to determine whether the conviction to tithe is a sincerely held religious belief (or giving of any amount to a church for that matter)? For example, what if the debtors feel convinced that tithing is required for Christians, but their church does not? Or, what if debtors are convinced that tithing on gross income is required, but their pastor thinks that tithing only on net income is required? Or, is it enough for the court to observe the debtors in order to determine their good faith with regard to charitable contributions to their church?

Does this type of determination put courts in an unusual and difficult position? Should we be concerned about that? In other words, do we want courts inquiring into the sincerity of religious beliefs or is that beyond the jurisdiction of the civil magistrate?

_____

_____

_____

_____

_____

CHAPTER 8
THE GM BANKRUPTCY

"In any moment of decision the best thing you can do is the right thing, the next best thing is the wrong thing, and the worst thing you can do is nothing."

Attributed to Theodore Roosevelt

"I said to my soul, be still, and wait without hope
For hope would be hope for the wrong thing."

East Coker by T. S. Eliot

In re General Motors Corp.
407 B.R. 463 (Bankr. S.D. N.Y. 2009)[1]

ROBERT E. GERBER, Bankruptcy Judge.

* * *

In this contested matter in the jointly administered chapter 11 cases of Debtors General Motors Corporation and certain of its subsidiaries (together, "**GM**"), the Debtors move for an order, pursuant to section 363 of the Bankruptcy Code, approving GM's sale of the bulk of its assets (the "**363 Transaction**"), pursuant to a "Master Sale and Purchase

---

[1] This opinion is 58-pages long in the Bankruptcy Reporter. Obviously, it has been heavily edited. The bolding of certain terms appears in the opinion itself.

Agreement" and related documents (the "**MPA**"), to Vehicle Acquisitions Holdings LLC (the "**Purchaser**")[2]—a purchaser sponsored by the U.S. Department of the Treasury (the "**U.S. Treasury**")—free and clear of liens, claims, encumbrances, and other interests. The Debtors also seek approval of the assumption and assignment of the executory contracts that would be needed by the Purchaser, and of a settlement with the United Auto Workers ("**UAW**") pursuant to an agreement (the "**UAW Settlement Agreement**") under which GM would satisfy obligations to an estimated 500,000 retirees.

GM's motion is supported by the Creditors' Committee; the U.S. Government (which has advanced approximately $50 billion to GM, and is GM's largest pre-and post-petition creditor); the Governments of Canada and Ontario (which ultimately will have advanced about $9.1 billion); the UAW (an affiliate of which is GM's single largest unsecured creditor); the indenture trustees for GM's approximately $27 billion in unsecured bonds; and an ad hoc committee representing holders of a majority of those bonds.

But the motion has engendered many objections and limited objections, by a variety of others. The objectors include, among others, a minority of the holders of GM's unsecured bonds (most significantly, an ad hoc committee of three of them (the "**F & D Bondholders Committee**"), holding approximately .01% of GM's bonds), who contend, among other things, that GM's assets can be sold only under a chapter 11 plan, and that the proposed section 363 sale amounts to an impermissible "*sub rosa*" plan.

Objectors and limited objectors also include tort litigants who object to provisions in the approval order limiting successor liability claims against the Purchaser; asbestos litigants with similar concerns, along with concerns as to asbestos ailments that have not yet been discovered; and non-UAW unions ("**Splinter Unions**") speaking for their retirees, concerned that the Purchaser does not plan to treat their retirees as well as the UAW's retirees.

On the most basic issue, whether a 363 sale is proper, GM contends that this is exactly the kind of case where a section 363 sale is appropriate and indeed essential—and where under the several rulings of the Second Circuit and the Supreme Court in this area, GM's business can be sold, and its value preserved, before the company dies. The Court agrees. GM cannot survive with its continuing losses and associated loss of liquidity, and without the governmental funding that will expire in a matter of days. And there are no options to this sale—especially any premised on the notion that the company could survive the process of negotiations and litigation that characterizes the plan confirmation process.

---

[2] When discussing the mechanics of the 363 Transaction, the existing GM will be referred to as "**Old GM,**" and the Purchaser will be referred to as "**New GM.**"

As nobody can seriously dispute, the only alternative to an immediate sale is liquidation—a disastrous result for GM's creditors, its employees, the suppliers who depend on GM for their own existence, and the communities in which GM operates. In the event of a liquidation, creditors now trying to increase their incremental recoveries would get nothing.

Neither the Code, nor the caselaw—especially the caselaw in the Second Circuit—requires waiting for the plan confirmation process to take its course when the inevitable consequence would be liquidation. Bankruptcy courts have the power to authorize sales of assets at a time when there still is value to preserve—to prevent the death of the patient on the operating table.

Nor can the Court accept various objectors' contention that there here is a *sub rosa* plan. GM's assets simply are being sold, with the consideration to GM to be hereafter distributed to stakeholders, consistent with their statutory priorities, under a subsequent plan. Arrangements that will be made by the Purchaser do not affect the distribution of the *Debtor's* property, and will address wholly different needs and concerns— arrangements that the Purchaser needs to create a new GM that will be lean and healthy enough to survive.

Issues as to how any approval order should address *successor liability* are the only truly debatable issues in this case. And while textual analysis is ultimately inconclusive and caselaw on a nationwide basis is not uniform, the Court believes in *stare decisis;* it follows the caselaw in this Circuit and District in holding that to the extent the Purchaser has not voluntarily agreed to accept successor liability, GM's property—like that of Chrysler, just a few weeks ago—may be sold free and clear of claims.

Those and other issues are addressed below. GM's motion is granted. The following are the Court's Findings of Fact, Conclusions of Law, and bases for the exercise of its discretion in connection with this determination.

Findings of Fact

* * *

1. Background

GM is primarily engaged in the worldwide production of cars, trucks, and parts. It is the largest Original Equipment Manufacturer ("**OEM**") in the U.S., and the second largest in the world.

GM has marketed cars and trucks under many brands—most of them household names in the U.S.—including Buick, Cadillac, Chevrolet,

Pontiac, GMC, Saab, Saturn, HUMMER, and Opel. It operates in virtually every country in the world.

GM maintains its executive offices in Detroit, Michigan, and its major financial and treasury operations in New York, New York. As of March 31, 2009, GM employed approximately 235,000 employees worldwide, of whom 163,000 were hourly employees and 72,000 were salaried. Of GM's 235,000 employees, approximately 91,000 are employed in the U.S. Approximately 62,000 (or 68%) of those U.S. employees were represented by unions as of March 31, 2009. The UAW represents by far the largest portion of GM's U.S. unionized employees, representing approximately 61,000 employees.

As of March 31, 2009, GM had consolidated reported global assets and liabilities of approximately $82 billion, and $172 billion, respectively. However, its assets appear on its balance sheet at book value, as contrasted to a value based on any kind of valuation or appraisal. And if GM had to be liquidated, its liquidation asset value, as discussed below, would be less than 10% of that $82 billion amount.

While GM has publicly traded common stock, no one in this chapter 11 case has seriously suggested that GM's stock is "in the money," or anywhere close to that. By any standard, there can be no doubt that GM is insolvent. In fact, as also discussed below, if GM were to liquidate, its unsecured creditors would receive nothing on their claims.

2. GM's Dealer Network

Substantially all of GM's worldwide car and truck deliveries (totaling 8.4 million vehicles in 2008) are marketed through independent retail dealers or distributors. GM relies heavily on its relationships with dealers, as substantially all of its retail sales are through its network of independent retail dealers and distributors.

The 363 Transaction contemplates the assumption by GM and the assignment to New GM of dealer franchise agreements relating to approximately 4,100 of its 6,000 dealerships, modified in ways to make GM more competitive (as modified, "**Participation Agreements**"). But GM cannot take all of the dealers on the same basis. At the remaining dealer's option, GM will either reject those agreements, or assume modified agreements, called "**Deferred Termination Agreements.**"

The Deferred Termination Agreements will provide dealers with whom GM cannot go forward a softer landing and orderly termination. GM is providing approximately 17 months' notice of termination.

As of the time of the hearing on this motion, approximately 99% of the continuing dealers had signed Participation Agreements and 99% of the dealers so affected had signed Deferred Termination Agreements.

The agreements of both types include waivers of rights that dealers would have in connection with their franchises. In accordance with a settlement with the Attorneys General of approximately 45 states (the "**AGs**"), the Debtors and the Purchaser agreed to modifications to the Purchase Agreement and the proposed approval order under which (subject to the more precise language in the proposed order) the Court makes no finding as to the extent any such modifications are enforceable, and any disputes as to that will be resolved locally.

3. GM's Suppliers

As the nation's largest automobile manufacturer, GM uses the services of thousands of suppliers—resulting in approximately $50 billion in annual supplier payments. In North America alone, GM uses a network of approximately 11,500 suppliers. In addition, there are over 600 suppliers whose sales to GM represent over 30% of their annual revenues. Thus hundreds, if not thousands, of automotive parts suppliers depend, either in whole or in part, on GM for survival.

4. GM's Financial Distress

Historically, GM was one of the best performing OEMs in the U.S. market. But with the growth of competitors with far lower cost structures and dramatically lower benefit obligations, GM's leadership position in the U.S. began to decline. At least as a result of that lower cost competition and market forces in the U.S. and abroad (including jumps in the price of gasoline; a massive recession (with global dislocation not seen since the 1930s); a dramatic decline in U.S. domestic auto sales; and a freeze-up in consumer and commercial credit markets), GM suffered a major drop in new vehicle sales and in market share—from 45% in 1980 to a forecast 19.5% in 2009.

The Court does not need to make further factual findings as to the many causes for GM's difficulties, and does not do so. Observers might differ as to the causes or opine that there were others as well, and might differ especially with respect to which causes were most important. But what is clear is that, especially in 2008 and 2009, GM suffered a steep erosion in revenues, significant operating losses, and a dramatic loss of liquidity, putting its future in grave jeopardy.

5. U.S. Government Assistance

By the fall of 2008, GM was in the midst of a severe liquidity crisis, and its ability to continue operations grew more and more uncertain with each passing day. As a result, in November 2008, GM was compelled to seek financial assistance from the U.S. Government.

The U.S. Government understood the draconian consequences of the situation—one that affected not just GM, but also Chrysler, and to a lesser extent, Ford (the "**Big Three**"). And the failure of any of the Big Three (or worse, more than one of them) might well bring grievous ruin on the thousands of suppliers to the Big Three (many of whom have already filed their own bankruptcy cases, in this District, Delaware, Michigan and elsewhere); other businesses in the communities where the Big Three operate; dealers throughout the country; and the states and municipalities who looked to the Big Three, their suppliers and their employees for tax revenues.

The U.S. Government's fear—a fear this Court shares, if GM cannot be saved as a going concern—was of a systemic failure throughout the domestic automotive industry and the significant harm to the overall U.S. economy that would result from the loss of hundreds of thousands of jobs and the sequential shutdown of hundreds of ancillary businesses if GM had to cease operations.

Thus in response to the troubles plaguing the American automotive industry, the U.S. Government, through the U.S. Treasury and its Presidential Task Force on the Auto Industry (the "**Auto Task Force**"), implemented various programs to support and stabilize the domestic automotive industry—including support for consumer warranties and direct loans. Thus at GM's request in late 2008, the U.S. Treasury determined to make available to GM billions of dollars in emergency secured financing in order to sustain GM's operations while GM developed a new business plan. At the time that the U.S. Treasury first extended credit to GM, there was absolutely no other source of financing available. No party other than Treasury conveyed its willingness to loan funds to GM and thereby enable it to continue operating.

The first loan came in December 2008, after GM submitted a proposed viability plan to Congress. That plan contemplated GM's shift to smaller, more fuel-efficient cars, a reduction in the number of GM brand names and dealerships, and a renegotiation of GM's agreement with its principal labor union. As part of its proposed plan, GM sought emergency funding in the form of an $18 billion federal loan.

But the U.S. Government was not of a mind to extend a loan that large, and after negotiations, the U.S. Treasury and GM entered into a term loan agreement on December 31, 2008 (the "**Treasury Prepetition Loan**"), that provided GM up to $13.4 billion in financing on a senior secured basis. Under that facility, GM immediately borrowed $4 billion, followed by $5.4 billion less than a month later, and the remaining $4 billion on February 17, 2009.

At the time this loan was made, GM was in very weak financial condition, and the loan was made under much better terms than could be obtained from any commercial lender—if any lender could have been found at all. But the Court has no doubt whatever, and finds, that the Treasury Prepetition Loan was intended to be, and was, a loan and not a contribution of equity. As contrasted with other TARP transactions that involved the U.S. Treasury making direct investments in troubled companies in return for common or preferred equity, the U.S. Treasury structured the Treasury Prepetition Loan as a loan with the only equity received by the U.S. Treasury being in the form of two warrants. The agreement had terms and covenants of a loan rather than an equity investment. The U.S. Treasury sought and received first liens on many assets, and second liens on other collateral. The transaction also had separate collateral documents. And the U.S. Treasury entered into intercreditor agreements with GM's other senior secured lenders in order to agree upon the secured lenders' respective prepetition priorities.

The Court further finds, as a fact or mixed question of fact and law, looking at the totality of the circumstances, that there was nothing inequitable about the way the U.S. Treasury behaved in advancing these funds. Nor did the U.S. Treasury act inequitably to GM's creditors, who were assisted, and not injured, by the U.S. Treasury's efforts to keep GM alive and to forestall a liquidation of the company.

GM had provided a business plan to Congress under which GM might restore itself to profitability, but it was widely perceived to be unsatisfactory. The U.S. Treasury required GM to submit a proposed business plan to demonstrate its future competitiveness that went significantly farther than the one GM had submitted to Congress. As conditions to the U.S. Treasury's willingness to provide financing, GM was to:

(i) reduce its approximately $27 billion in unsecured public debt by no less than two-thirds;

(ii) reduce its total compensation to U.S. employees so that by no later than December 31, 2009, such compensation would be competitive with Nissan, Toyota, or Honda in the U.S.;

(iii) eliminate compensation or benefits to employees who had been discharged, furloughed, or idled, other than customary severance pay;

(iv) apply, by December 31, 2009, work rules for U.S. employees in a manner that would be competitive with the work rules for employees of Nissan, Toyota, or Honda in the U.S.; and

(v) make at least half of the $20 billion contribution that GM was obligated to make to a VEBA[3] Trust for UAW retirees ("**VEBA Trust**") in the form of common stock, rather than cash.

Thereafter, in March 2009, Treasury indicated that if GM was unable to complete an effective out-of-court restructuring, it should consider a new, more aggressive, viability plan under an expedited Court-supervised process to avoid further erosion of value. In short, GM was to file a bankruptcy petition and take prompt measures to preserve its value while there was still value to save.

The Treasury Prepetition Loan agreement (whose formal name was "Loan and Security Agreement," or "**LSA**") provided that, if, by March 31, 2009, the President's designee hadn't issued a certification that GM had taken all steps necessary to achieve long-term viability, then the loans due to Treasury would become due and payable 30 days thereafter. And on March 30, the President announced that the viability plan proposed by GM was not satisfactory, and didn't justify a substantial new investment of taxpayer dollars.

But rather than leaving GM to simply go into liquidation, the President stated that the U.S. Government would provide assistance to avoid such a result, *if* GM took the necessary additional steps to justify that assistance—including reaching agreements with the UAW, GM's bondholders, and the VEBA Trust. The conditions to federal assistance required substantial debt reduction and the submission of a revised business plan that was more aggressive in both scope and timing.

As an alternative to liquidation, the President indicated that the U.S. Treasury would extend to GM adequate working capital for a period of another 60 days to enable it to continue operations. And as GM's largest secured creditor, the U.S. Treasury would negotiate with GM to develop and implement a more aggressive and comprehensive viability plan. The President also stated that GM needed a "fresh start to implement the restructuring plan," which "may mean using our [B]ankruptcy [C]ode as a mechanism to help [it] restructure quickly and emerge stronger." The President explained:

> What I'm talking about is using our existing legal structure as a tool that, with the backing of the U.S. Government, can make it easier for General Motors . . . to *quickly* clear away old debts that are weighing [it] down so

---

[3] GM has used trusts qualified as "voluntary employee beneficiary associations" under the Internal Revenue Code (each, a "**VEBA**"), to hold reserves to meet GM's future obligations to provide healthcare and life insurance benefits ("**OPEB**") to its salaried and hourly employees upon retirement. In substance, the employer makes contributions to the VEBA, and the VEBA funds the health benefits to the retirees.

that [it] can get back on [its] feet and onto a path to success;
a tool that we can use, even as workers stay on the job
building cars that are being sold.

What I'm not talking about is a process where a
company is simply broken up, sold off, and no longer exists.
We're not talking about that. And what I'm *not talking about
is a company that's stuck in court for years, unable to get out.*[4]

The U.S. Treasury and GM subsequently entered into amended
credit agreements for the Treasury Prepetition Loan to provide for an
additional $2 billion in financing that GM borrowed on April 24, 2009, and
another $4 billion that GM borrowed on May 20, 2009. The funds
advanced to GM under the Treasury Prepetition Loan—ultimately $19.4
billion in total (all on a senior secured basis)—permitted GM to survive
through the date of the filing of its bankruptcy case.

On June 1, 2009 (the "**Filing Date**"), GM filed its chapter 11
petition in this Court.

6. GM's First Quarter Results

[Suffice it to say that GM's first quarter results, which are here
omitted, were horrible.]

7. The 363 Transaction

As noted above, in connection with providing financing, Treasury
advised GM that, if an out-of-court restructuring was not possible, GM
should consider the bankruptcy process. That would enable GM to
implement a transaction under which substantially all GM's assets would
be purchased by a Treasury-sponsored purchaser (subject to any higher or
better offer), in an expedited process under section 363 of the Code.

Under this game plan, the Purchaser would acquire the purchased
assets; create a New GM; and operate New GM free of any entanglement
with the bankruptcy cases. If the sale could be accomplished quickly
enough, before GM's value dissipated as a result of continuing losses and
consumer uncertainty, the 363 sale would thereby preserve the going
concern value; avoid systemic failure; provide continuing employment;
protect the many communities dependent upon the continuation of GM's
business, and restore consumer confidence.

To facilitate the process, the U.S. Treasury and the governments of
Canada and Ontario (through their Export Development Canada ("**EDC**"))
agreed to provide DIP financing for GM through the chapter 11 process.

---

[4] Emphasis added here by the Court.

But they would provide the DIP financing *only* if the sale of the purchased assets occurred on an *expedited* basis. That condition was imposed to:

(i) preserve the value of the business;
(ii) restore (or at least minimize further loss of) consumer confidence;
(iii) mitigate the increasing damage that GM itself, and the industry, would suffer if GM's major business operations were to remain in bankruptcy; and
(iv) avoid the enormous costs of financing a lengthy chapter 11 case. Treasury also agreed to provide New GM with adequate post-acquisition financing.

Importantly, the DIP financing to be furnished by the U.S. Treasury and EDC is the only financing that is available to GM. The U.S. Treasury (with its Canadian EDC co-lender) is the only entity that is willing to extend DIP financing to GM. Other efforts to obtain such financing have been unsuccessful. Absent adequate DIP financing, GM will have no choice but to liquidate. But the U.S. Government has stated it will not provide DIP financing without the 363 Transaction, and the DIP financing will come to an end if the 363 Transaction is not approved by July 10. Without such financing, these cases will plunge into a liquidation.

Alternatives to a sale have turned out to be unsuccessful, and offer no hope of success now. In accordance with standard section 363 practice, the 363 Transaction was subject to higher and better offers, but none were forthcoming. The Court finds this hardly surprising. Only the U.S. and Canadian Governmental authorities were prepared to invest in GM—and then not so much by reason of the economic merit of the purchase, but rather to address the underlying societal interests in preserving jobs and the North American auto industry, the thousands of suppliers to that industry, and the health of the communities, in the U.S. and Canada, in which GM operates.

In light of GM's substantial secured indebtedness, approximately $50 billion, the only entity that has the financial wherewithal and is qualified to purchase the assets—and the only entity that has stepped forward to make such a purchase—is the U.S. Treasury-sponsored Purchaser. But the Purchaser is willing to proceed only under an expedited sale process under the Bankruptcy Code.

8. The Liquidation Alternative

In connection with its consideration of alternatives, GM secured an analysis (the "**Liquidation Analysis**"), prepared by AlixPartners LLP, of what GM's assets would be worth in a liquidation. The Liquidation Analysis concluded that the realizable value of the assets of GM (net of the costs of liquidation) would range between approximately $6 billion and $10 billion. No evidence has been submitted to the contrary. This was in the context of an assumed $116.5 billion in general unsecured claims, though this could increase with lease and contract rejection claims and pension termination claims.

While the Liquidation Analysis projected some recoveries for secured debt and administrative and priority claims, it concluded that there would be *no recovery whatsoever* for unsecured creditors. The Court has no basis to doubt those conclusions. The Court finds that in the event of a liquidation, unsecured creditors would recover nothing.

9. Fairness of the Transaction

Before the 363 Transaction was presented for Court approval, GM's Board of Directors (the "**Board**") (all but one of whose members were independent, and advised by the law firm of Cravath, Swaine & Moore), received a fairness opinion, dated May 31, 2009 (the "**Fairness Opinion**"), from Evercore Group L.L.C. ("**Evercore**").

The Fairness Opinion's conclusion was that the purchase price was fair to GM, from a financial point of view. No contrary evidence has been submitted to the Court.

10. Specifics of the Transaction

The sale transaction, as embodied in the MPA and related documents, is complex. Its "deal points" can be summarized as follows:

(a) Acquired and Excluded Assets

Under the Sale, New GM will acquire all of Old GM's assets, with the exception of certain assets expressly excluded under the MPA (respectively, the "**Purchased Assets**" and the "**Excluded Assets**"). . . .

(b) Assumed and Excluded Liabilities

Old GM will retain all liabilities except those defined in the MPA as "**Assumed Liabilities**." The Assumed Liabilities include:

> (i) product liability claims arising out of products delivered at or after the Sale transaction closes (the "***Closing***");
> (ii) the warranty and recall obligations of both Old GM and New GM;

(iii) all employment-related obligations and liabilities under any assumed employee benefit plan relating to employees that are or were covered by the UAW collective bargaining agreement;

and—by reason of an important change that was made in the MPA after the filing of the motion—

(iv) broadening the first category substantially, *all* product liability claims arising from accidents or other discrete incidents arising from operation of GM vehicles occurring subsequent to the closing of the 363 Transaction, *regardless of when the product was purchased.*

The liabilities being retained by Old GM include:

(i) product liability claims arising out of products delivered prior to the Closing (to the extent they weren't assumed by reason of the change in the MPA after the filing of objections);

(ii) liabilities for claims arising out of exposure to asbestos;

(iii) liabilities to third parties for claims based upon "[c]ontract, tort or any other basis";

(iv) liabilities related to any implied warranty or other implied obligation arising under statutory or common law; and

(v) employment-related obligations not otherwise assumed, including, among other obligations, those arising out of the employment, potential employment, or termination of any individual (other than an employee covered by the UAW collective bargaining agreement) prior to or at the Closing.

(c) Consideration

Old GM is to receive consideration estimated to be worth approximately $45 billion, plus the value of equity interests that it will receive in New GM. It will come in the following forms:

(i) a credit bid by the U.S. Treasury and EDC, who will credit bid the majority of the indebtedness outstanding under their DIP facility and the Treasury Prepetition Loan;

(ii) the assumption by New GM of approximately $6.7 billion of indebtedness under the DIP facilities, plus an additional $1.175 billion to be advanced by the U.S. Treasury under a new DIP facility (the "**Wind Down Facility**") whose proceeds will be used by Old GM to wind down its affairs;

(iii) the surrender of the warrant that had been issued by Old GM to Treasury in connection with the Treasury Prepetition Loan;

(iv) 10% of the post-closing outstanding shares of New GM, plus an additional 2% if the estimated amount of allowed prepetition general unsecured claims against Old GM exceeds $35 billion;

(v) two warrants, each to purchase 7.5% of the post-closing outstanding shares of New GM, with an exercise price based on a $15 billion equity valuation and a $30 billion equity valuation, respectively; and

(vi) the assumption of liabilities, including those noted above.

(d) Ownership of New GM

Under the terms of the Sale, New GM will be owned by four entities.

(i) Treasury will own 60.8% of New GM's common stock on an undiluted basis. It also will own $2.1 billion of New GM Series A Preferred Stock;

(ii) EDC will own 11.7% of New GM's common stock on an undiluted basis. It also will own $400 million of New GM Series A Preferred Stock;

(iii) A New Employees' Beneficiary Association Trust ("**New VEBA**") will own 17.5% of New GM's common stock on an undiluted basis. It also will own $6.5 billion of New GM's Series A Preferred Stock, and a 6–year warrant to acquire 2.5% of New GM's common stock, with an exercise price based on $75 billion total equity value; and

(iv) Finally, if a chapter 11 plan is implemented as contemplated under the structure of the Sale transaction, Old GM will own 10% of New GM's common stock on an undiluted basis. In addition, if the allowed prepetition general unsecured claims against Old GM exceed $35 billion, Old GM will be issued an additional 10 million shares, amounting to approximately 2% of New GM's common stock. Old GM will also own the two warrants mentioned above.

(e) Other Aspects of Transaction

New GM will make an offer of employment to all of the Sellers' non-unionized employees and unionized employees represented by the UAW. Substantially all of old GM's executory contracts with direct suppliers are likely to be assumed and assigned to New GM.

After the Closing, New GM will assume all liabilities arising under express written emission and limited warranties delivered in connection with the sale of new vehicles or parts manufactured or sold by Old GM.

One of the requirements of the U.S. Treasury, imposed when the Treasury Prepetition Loan was put in place, was the need to negotiate a new collective bargaining agreement which would allow GM to be fully competitive, and "equitize"—*i.e.*, convert to equity—at least one half of the obligation GM had to the UAW VEBA. Ultimately GM did so. New GM will make future contributions to the New VEBA that will provide retiree health and welfare benefits to former UAW employees and their spouses. Also, as part of the 363 Transaction, New GM will be the assignee of revised collective bargaining agreements with the UAW, the terms of which were recently ratified—though contingent upon the approval of the entirety of these motions.

* * *

12. Agreement with UAW

Workers in the U.S. do not have government provided healthcare benefits of the type that the employees of many of GM's foreign competitors do. Over the years, GM and the other members of the Big Three committed themselves to offer many of those healthcare benefits, resulting in decreased competitiveness and enormous liabilities. GM tried to reduce the costs of healthcare benefits for its employees, but these costs continued to substantially escalate. Many of these costs were in the form of obligations to pay healthcare costs of union employees on retirement.

In 2007 and 2008, GM settled various controversies with respect to its healthcare obligations by entering into an agreement (the "**2008 UAW Settlement Agreement**"), generally providing that responsibility for providing retiree healthcare would permanently shift from GM to a new plan that was independent of GM. GM would no longer have to pay for the benefits themselves, but instead would have to make specified contributions aggregating approximately $20.56 billion to be made by GM into the VEBA Trust. The 2008 UAW Settlement Agreement, therefore, fixed and capped GM's obligations—but in a very large amount.

As part of the 363 Transaction, the Purchaser and the UAW have reached a resolution addressing the ongoing provision of those benefits. New GM will make contributions to the New VEBA, which will have the obligation to fund the UAW retiree health and welfare benefits. And under the "**UAW Retiree Settlement Agreement**," New GM will put value into the New VEBA, which will then have the obligation to fund retiree medical benefits for the Debtors' retirees and surviving spouses represented by the UAW (the "**UAW–Represented Retirees**").

New GM will also assume modified and duly ratified collective bargaining agreements entered into by and between the Debtors and the UAW.

13. Need for Speed

GM and the U.S. Treasury say that the 363 Transaction must be approved and completed quickly. The Court finds that they are right.

* * *

14. Ultimate Facts

The Court thus makes the following findings of ultimate facts:

1. There is a good business reason for proceeding with the 363 Transaction now, as contrasted to awaiting the formulation and confirmation of a chapter 11 plan.
2. There is an articulated business justification for proceeding with the 363 Transaction now.
3. The 363 Transaction is an appropriate exercise of business judgment.
4. The 363 Transaction is the only available means to preserve the continuation of GM's business.
5. The 363 Transaction is the only available means to maximize the value of GM's business.
6. There is no viable alternative to the 363 Transaction.
7. The only alternative to the 363 Transaction is liquidation.
8. No unsecured creditor will here get less than it would receive in a liquidation.
9. The UAW Settlement is fair and equitable, and is in the best interests of both the estate and UAW members.
10. The secured debt owing to the U.S. Government and EDC (both post-petition and, to the extent applicable, prepetition) is not subject to recharacterization as equity or equitable subordination, and could be used for a credit bid.
11. The Purchaser is a purchaser in good faith.

* * *

NOTES AND QUESTIONS

1. The Controversy. During the so-called "Great Recession" following the financial collapse that began in late 2007, the United States government intervened in the United States economy in astounding ways unseen since the era of the Great Depression. The bailout and subsequent government-guided bankruptcy of General Motors Corporation is a controversial example of such intervention.

Many people argued, felt, and probably still feel that, given such a time of crisis, something had to be done and that this something (the government bailouts followed by the government-guided bankruptcy) was the best thing that could be done under the circumstances. Others argued, felt, and probably still feel that GM was not entitled to special government favors not open to other companies. The role of the government, it is argued, is not to pick winners and losers in the economy. It should remain uninvolved rather than intervening specially to prop up some favored yet failing companies while allowing others to fail.[5]

Perhaps now it is beginning to come clear why this chapter began with the two quotes that it did. The first, by President Theodore Roosevelt, indicates that doing nothing in any moment of decision is the worst option possible. Doing nothing in the financial crisis would have likely meant bankruptcy and collapse for the United States auto industry. GM would have entered bankruptcy like any other company, and it would have very likely lead to the destruction of the United States auto industry as we know it.[6] Whether a newer and stronger auto industry would have emerged like a phoenix rising from its ashes is a question to which we will never know the answer. Most Americans probably felt the risk was too great, and government intervention to save the auto industry was required. To do nothing was viewed as the worst option.

The second quote, by T. S. Eliot, demonstrates an alternative position. It calls for doing nothing and waiting. In fact, it cautions against even hoping as the hoping would be in the wrong thing. Some felt that the hope of saving GM was hope in the wrong thing. Over the years, GM (and indeed all of the big three automakers) made a number of mistakes that proved very costly. These mistakes, such as the huge salaries and enormous costly benefit plans promised to current and retired workers, resulted in it being virtually impossible for GM to remain competitive.[7] Companies that make mistakes like that, some feel, should be made to suffer the consequences up to and including going out of business. While the failure of these companies is painful, it ultimately leads to a stronger economy as stronger, financially-healthier, more

---

[5] Obviously, many, many businesses failed during the financial crisis and ensuing Great Recession. However, only certain businesses were "bailed out."

[6] The other members of the "Big Three" automakers, Chrysler and, to a lesser extent, Ford, also received government assistance during the financial crisis. Chrysler also benefited from a special bankruptcy arrangement very similar to GM's.

[7] At one point, 19 cents of every dollar made by GM went to pay so-called legacy costs, i.e., the costs of retirement, health insurance, and other benefits promised to retired GM workers. Accordingly, 19 cents of every dollar went to compensate workers who were no longer working.

innovative companies take the place of the weaker ones. Thus, some thought doing nothing was the best option.

What do you think should have been done? What would you have done if you were President? Would you have bailed out GM (and the various other companies that received government assistance during this period) or would you have done nothing?

---

2. Who Won? Who do you think benefited the most from the 363 Transaction and related plan? Who were GM's unsecured creditors, who the court says would get nothing under the plan? Unsecured creditors often get nothing or very little in bankruptcy, so why was GM so unique and important? Why were certain GM unsecured creditors entitled to special treatment?

---

3. The Civil Magistrate as Lender of Last Resort and Business Owner? Does the biblical role of the civil magistrate include being a lender of last resort and business owner? In other words, is bailing out companies and providing them with special privileges in bankruptcy within the biblical role of the civil magistrate? If not, is it justified because the company is really important to the national economy? What if instead the company's constituents (like the UAW) are really important and powerful politically?

Assuming for the moment that it is within the biblical jurisdiction of the civil magistrate, is it just to act in this role for one company while refusing to do to so for others? Or what about individuals, such as homeowners who are behind on their mortgages? If GM is entitled to special financing and special treatment in bankruptcy, should the government also provide such special financing and treatment to troubled American homeowners? Again, is importance to the economy or political power sufficient grounds to provide government favors to one group while withholding them from others who are deemed less important (whether economically or politically)? *See* Roger Bern, *A Biblical Model for Analysis of Issues of Law and Public Policy: with Illustrative Applications to Contracts, Antitrust, Remedies and Public Policy Issues*, 6 REGENT U. L. REV. 103, 110-131 (1995).

Index

A

Abraham 70
Apostle 19
Athens 14, 18
atonement 50
attorney 58, 64
attorneys 56, 72, 81
auto 1, 61, 78, 81-82, 86, 92
automakers 92

B

bailout 91-92
bankruptcy viii, xi, 1, 37-41, 43-45,
    51-53, 55-65, 67, 69, 71-72, 75-77, 79,
    81-87, 89, 91-93
BAPCPA 47-48, 51-53
Bern 22, 94
Bible vii, 2, 4-7, 9-11, 19-20, 22-25, 35-36,
    38-40, 42-44, 49-51, 53, 75
biblical viii, xi, 1-7, 9, 11, 13-14, 22-23, 27,
    29, 31, 33, 35-37, 39-41, 43-45, 48-53, 55,
    57, 59, 61, 63-64, 75, 93-94
bondservant 41-43
bondservice 42-43, 49, 64
borrowing 2-11, 38
breach 20-22, 27, 30-36
Brunner 58-60, 62
Burkett 5-7, 9-11
business 5-6, 9, 19-21, 23, 33, 37, 78, 82-86,
    91-93

C

charitable 65-76
Christ iii, 1, 49-51, 63
Christian vii-viii, 2-5, 9, 11, 17, 19, 24, 27,
    37-38, 40, 43-44, 52-53, 75-76
Christianity 15, 17
Colossians 19, 38, 50
commercial viii, xi, 13-25, 27, 30-32, 36-37,
    81, 83
contribute 66, 68
contributed 14, 70
contribution 65-74, 83-84
contributions 65-76, 84, 90
Corinthians 63, 75
credit 1, 21-22, 27-28, 31, 35, 55, 57, 59, 61,
    81-82, 85, 88, 91
creditor A, i-ii, vii-viii, x, 1-2, 4, 6, 8-11,
    13-14, 16, 18, 20, 22-24, 27-28, 30, 32-40,
    42, 44, 48, 50, 52, 56, 58, 60, 62, 64, 66-68,
    70, 72, 74, 76, 78, 80, 82, 84, 86, 88, 90-92,
    94
creditors 3, 21-22, 25, 31, 39, 43, 47, 51-52,
    65-66, 68-69, 72-74, 78-80, 83, 87, 93
crisis 19, 61, 81, 92

D

debt iii, viii, xi, 1-7, 9-11, 23, 35-36, 38-45,
    47-53, 55, 57-58, 60-61, 63-64, 70, 72-73,
    83-84, 87, 91
debtor A, i-ii, vii-viii, x, 1-2, 4, 6, 8-11, 13-14,
    16, 18-25, 27-28, 30-32, 34-40, 42-44,
    47-52, 56, 58-82, 84, 86, 88, 90, 92, 94
Deuteronomy 3, 6, 10, 19-20, 22, 25, 40, 42,
    49, 52, 64, 75

discharge 44, 47, 55, 57, 60-61, 63-64, 70, 73
dischargeability 62-63
dischargeable 44, 55
disobedience 39

E

element 32-33, 48
elements 33, 62-63
enslaved 49
Ephesians 19, 38
Exodus 19-20, 23, 38, 42

F

factor 62, 71
factors 21, 32-33, 59-60, 62-63, 71-72
faith 19, 48, 50, 55, 58-60, 62, 66, 69-74, 76, 91
financial 3, 19, 29, 37-40, 47, 55, 57, 59, 62, 67, 80-83, 86-87, 91-92

G

general 4-6, 10, 13-18, 20, 22-24, 31-32, 36, 42, 51, 58, 77, 81, 84, 87, 89, 92
generous 9, 47, 65, 74
gift 2, 6, 11, 69
gifts 57, 65, 75
GM xi, 77-93
good viii-ix, 1-2, 11, 14-15, 18, 20, 24-25, 30, 35, 38, 53, 55, 58-60, 62, 66, 69-74, 76, 91
gospel 49-51, 53, 63
Gothard 2-3, 5-6, 9, 11
government 1, 5, 15-16, 36, 61, 78, 81-82, 84, 86, 90-93
governments 1, 78, 85
grace 38-39, 42, 49
Grudem 6-9, 11, 19
guarantor 10, 24
guaranty 16, 24

H

Hebrews v, 70, 75

I

illegal 25
indebtedness 50, 86, 88

J

james 3, 14, 20-22
Jesus iii, 49-51, 63
john 16, 42, 49-50, 63, 75

K

Kings 64
Krischner 65, 75

L

law A, i-ii, v, vii-viii, x-xi, 1-2, 4, 6-11, 13-25,
    27-28, 30-32, 34-38, 40-45, 47-50, 52-53,
    55-60, 62, 64-66, 68-70, 72, 74-76, 78-80,
    82-84, 86-88, 90, 92, 94
lawyer viii
lawyers viii-ix, 16, 56
legal viii, 2, 10, 15-17, 20, 23-25, 37, 40,
    43-44, 49-50, 58-59, 69, 84
legally 40
lend 3, 8-9, 40, 52
lender 2-4, 7, 22, 52, 83, 86, 93
lenders 9, 36, 39, 52, 83
lendeth 40
lending 2, 6-8, 11
Leviticus 19, 38, 42, 64, 75
loan 1, 3, 6, 24, 28-30, 33-35, 44, 47, 52,
    56-58, 60-62, 82-85, 88-89
loans 1, 10, 35-36, 44, 55-62, 82, 84
love ix-x, 3-4, 7, 9, 39, 41
Luke 14, 49, 75

M

magistrate 22-23, 25, 36, 76, 93
Marlow 55-61, 64
Matthew 14, 19, 38, 50, 75
merchant 13-14, 19
merchants 19-20
mercy 6, 38-39, 42
Micah 19
Motors 77, 84, 92

N

necessary 6, 20, 27, 32-33, 42, 64-70, 72, 75,

84
nondischargeability xi, 55, 57, 59, 61, 63-64
nondischargeable 73

O

obedience 39
obedient 7, 38, 49

P

paralegal vii, 56, 59
particular viii, 5, 10, 14-16, 18-19, 21, 34, 42,
    44, 51-52
particulars 10
peace 20-22, 27, 30-36, 70
plan 18, 23, 29, 60, 65-74, 78-79, 82-85,
    88-91, 93
pledge 19-20, 22, 25
pledgeable 20
pledged 28, 30, 32
pledges 20
political viii, 1, 56, 93
politically 93-94
politics 14, 37
principle 13-15, 17, 20-22, 36, 47-48, 51
principles v, 2, 5-6, 9-10, 13-18, 20, 22-24,
    27, 35-36, 52
property 4, 19-21, 28-36, 66, 71, 73, 79
Proverbs 3, 5-6, 10, 19, 24, 38
Psalm 6, 9, 38
purpose vii, 31, 48, 50-53, 64, 69, 72
purposes xi, 5, 23, 43, 47, 49, 51, 53, 66

systems viii, 1, 11, 16, 43, 52, 63-64

R

reasonably 32, 34, 52, 65-70, 73, 75
recession 81, 91-92
Reformation 19
relief 11, 38, 40-45, 48-53, 55, 57, 60, 63, 67, 72
religion 19
religious 4, 66-67, 69-70, 72, 76
repossess 20-21, 23, 28, 30-31, 33-34
repossessed 28-29, 35
repossessing 21
repossession xi, 13-14, 19-22, 27-36
repossessor 36
repossessors 29-30, 32
Romans v, 3, 5-7, 19, 22, 49
Rushdoony 3-6, 9, 11, 22, 42, 48-49, 75

S

Sabbath 4, 41-43, 48-52
sabbatical 6, 42
Salisbury 21, 27-34
salvation 51, 63
Scripture ii, v, 2-4, 6, 9, 19, 27
secured 13, 20-23, 25, 27, 30-31, 34-35, 82-87, 91
security 19-20, 28, 34, 84
self-help 14, 21, 27, 31, 35
sin viii, 1-6, 8, 11, 37-39, 41, 43, 49-51, 63
slave 4, 7, 41, 49-50
slavery 4-5, 42, 49-51
society 4, 8, 20, 22, 31, 34, 43-44, 52-53, 62-63, 75
statute 30-32, 65
statutes 3, 31
student vii, 1, 44, 55-62
surety 6, 10, 24-25
system ii, 2, 11, 23-25, 37-38, 40, 42-45, 48-53, 63-64

T

Tabb 47
theology 4
tithe 75-76
tithes 65, 74-76
tithing xi, 65, 67, 69, 71, 73, 75-76
Tuomala 15-19

U

unsecured 27, 57, 66-67, 70, 72-73, 78, 80, 83, 87, 89, 91, 93

W

worldview vii-viii, xi, 1-2, 11, 13, 18, 27, 55, 57, 59, 61, 63

CPSIA information can be obtained
at www.ICGtesting.com
Printed in the USA
LVHW061504050821
694475LV00005B/73